CATHOLICS AND THE AMERICAN POLITY

CATHOLICS
AND THE
American Polity

✤ ✤ ✤

Approaches & Contestations

EDITED BY
PIETER VREE
AND
THOMAS STORCK

AROUCA
PRESS

ISBN: 978-1-998492-58-9 (pbk)
ISBN: 978-1-998492-59-6 (hc)

Cover design by
Julian Kwasniewski

To my father, Dale, a great man
— *Pieter Vree*

CONTENTS

Introduction, *Pieter Vree* xi

Acknowledgements xviii

1   America is an Epic Comedy—We Just Caught the
Bus in Time, *Virginia L. Arbery* 1

2   A Less Prominent Place, Perhaps, but Still a Place
from which to Serve, *Casey Chalk* 8

3   "Stuck Inside of Mobile With the Memphis Blues
Again," *Will Hoyt* 15

4   A Permanent Seat on the Right Side of the Table,
George Hawley 19

5   Strike the Shepherd and the Sheep Will Be Scattered,
Kan Ito 24

6   Zoomer Catholics: A Hopeful Sign, a Future
Aborning, *A. James McAdams* 26

7   A Laughable Proposition, *Preston R. Simpson* 31

8   Moral Credibility and the Temptation to Power,
Mark Barrett 34

9   No Faith, No Future, *Charles A. Coulombe* 38

10   "The Future's so Bright...", *Christopher Beiting* . . 42

11   Decision and Indecision, Hope and Hopelessness,
Karl Keating 49

12   Orthodoxy and Beauty—Forget the Rest,
Gracjan Kraszewski 53

13   The Ship Is Sinking—Man the Lifeboats!,
Jude Russo 60

14   Building a Catholic Force to be Reckoned With:
A Blueprint, *Marek Jan Chodakiewicz* 66

15 Catholic Organization: A Universal Vision of
Both Word and Deed, *Christopher Zehnder* 70

16 Pipedreaming about Political Power Plays,
John M. Grondelski. 76

17 Living the Gospel in a Milieu of Arrogant Secularism,
James G. Hanink 79

18 Integralism: A Non-Individualistic Understanding
of Human Life, *Edmund Waldstein, O.Cist.*. 84

19 Catholic Existence in a Protestant Experiment,
Thomas Storck. 91

20 Against Apocalyptic Whiggism, *Edwin Dyga* 98

21 The Kingship of Christ and the Catholic
Counterworld, *Robert McTeigue, S.J.* 105

22 The Strange Soul of Our Secularist Empire,
Jason M. Morgan. 112

23 America Possessed: The Demon of Counterfeit
Reality, *Thaddeus Kozinski* 118

24 Casting Down the Mighty, Lifting Up the Lowly,
John C. Médaille 124

25 What We Are Doing vs. What We Should Be Doing,
Al Kresta. 130

AFTERWORD, *Thomas Storck.* 135

INTRODUCTION
PIETER VREE

EORGE WASHINGTON, IN HIS FIRST inaugural address, called the "republican model of government" an "experiment entrusted to the hands of the American people." Today, the American people's hands are increasingly at one another's throats. Gone are the days of trying to "just get along." Polarization is the defining characteristic of our politics. In the past few years, we've witnessed politically motivated takeovers of civic and educational buildings, riots and the destruction of downtown districts, and assassinations and assassination attempts. This politics-as-bloodsport takes place against a backdrop of shouting matches on television news shows, in legislative arenas, and on college campuses.

Not surprisingly, a pall has settled over the land of the free. Those not heavily invested are growing weary of the ideological clashes. A 2023 Pew Research poll found that nearly two-thirds of Americans feel "exhausted" when thinking about politics. By contrast, a mere ten percent feel "hopeful." Even fewer (four percent) feel "excited."[1] Concurrently, there's a rising dissatisfaction with our republican model of government. An earlier poll found that eighty-five percent of Americans say our political system is in need of "major changes" or must be "completely reformed."[2]

Amid the general discontent stands a people long perceived by many Americans as outsiders, natural nonconformists.

---

[1] "Americans' Dismal Views of the Nation's Politics," Pew Research Center (Sept. 19, 2023), https://www.pewresearch.org/politics/2023/09/19/americans-dismal-views-of-the-nations-politics.

[2] "Citizens in Advanced Economies Want Significant Changes to Their Political Systems," Pew Research Center (Oct. 21, 2021), https://www.pewresearch.org/global/2021/10/21/citizens-in-advanced-economies-want-significant-changes-to-their-political-systems.

It's no great revelation to say that Catholics have never been at home in these United States. Indeed, one of the distinguishing marks of American history is the perdurance of anti-Catholicism. It has been called "the deepest bias in the history of the American people" (by Arthur Schlesinger Jr.) and "the last acceptable prejudice" (by Philip Jenkins). In fact, anti-Catholicism could be said to be foundational to the American "experiment." Its roots run deep. The ideas of John Locke, the British philosopher widely acknowledged as the father of liberalism, greatly influenced the American founding; Thomas Jefferson praised him as one of the "three greatest men that have lived, without exception."[3] Locke had a distinctive anti-Catholic streak. "Papists," he wrote, "are not to enjoy the benefit of toleration." Why not? Because their ideas are "absolutely destructive to all governments but the pope's." When persecuted, Locke went on to say, Catholics are "less apt to be pitied than others."[4]

Pitied they haven't been. Not here. From the Blaine Amendments to the Obama administration's battles with the Little Sisters of the Poor, from the Ku Klux Klan and the Know-Nothings to Antifa and Jane's Revenge, rulers from above and ruffians from below have sought to marginalize Catholics in public life. To put it in biblical terms, they have tried to cast out Catholics from the banquet and banish them to the outer darkness.

An episode from as recently as 1990 is illustrative of this phenomenon.[5] John Cardinal O'Connor, then-archbishop of New York, wrote in his archdiocesan newspaper that Catholics who advocate pro-abortion legislation are at risk of excommunication. This caught the eye of the press (back when the press paid attention to what Catholic prelates wrote), and the cardinal found himself firmly in the

---

[3] Thomas Jefferson, letter to John Trumbull (Feb. 15, 1789).
[4] John Locke, *Essay on Toleration* (1667).
[5] The following cited in: Kenneth R. Craycraft Jr., *The American Myth of Religious Freedom* (Dallas, TX: Spence Publishing Company, 1999), pp. 13–15.

crosshairs. *The New York Times* accused him of "tearing at the truce of tolerance that permits America's pluralist democracy to work." The *Washington Post* likewise accused him of doing "damage to religious tolerance." Worst was what appeared in the *Philadelphia Inquirer*. Columnist David Boldt had the temerity to warn Cardinal O'Connor that his articulation of basic Catholic teaching — to a Catholic audience! — risked "reawakening all the old religious prejudices and fears that once inflamed American politics." In other words, keep your mouth shut, big guy, or you'll get what's coming to you.

To drive home the point that Catholic beliefs have no place in the public square, Boldt wrote, "The Roman Catholic Church, it needs to be remembered, is quite literally an un-American institution.... [Its] views are sharply at odds with those that inform the laws of American secular society."

Ever since that epic shout down, the Church has been reeling. The self-inflicted sex-abuse scandals that erupted in the early 2000s further damaged the Catholic cause. Priests have become objects of mockery and derision in the public mind, bishops have effectively lost their moral authority, and the share of Catholics among the general population has steadily diminished. As institutional influence wanes, expressions and acts of anti-Catholicism surge. They often manifest in strange and surprising ways, as, for example, intolerance in the halls of power — Senator Dianne Feinstein expressed "concern" that "the dogma lives loudly" in Amy Coney Barrett, a Catholic mother of seven, during her 2017 Supreme Court confirmation hearings — and violence in the public arena — the FBI recorded ninety-seven incidents of anti-Catholic hate crimes in 2021 alone, and there were four hundred and eighteen attacks on Catholic churches from 2021 to 2024.[6]

---

[6] Federal Bureau of Investigation, *Supplemental Hate Crime Statistics, 2021*, Table 1A (March 2023); Catholic Vote, *Violence Tracker*, https:// catholicvote.org/tracker-church-attacks.

The antagonism to which Catholics are subject today coincides with a larger phenomenon: the collapse of religion as a cultural force. Financial and sexual scandals have beset both Protestant and Catholic institutions, and the number of pew-sitters has plummeted across all confessions. According to data from Gallup, only thirty percent of self-professed Protestants attended weekly services in 2023. Even among Muslims, attendance has dropped; only twenty-eight percent attend mosque on a weekly basis. But the biggest drop has been among Catholics, only twenty-three percent of whom attend Mass once a week.[7] Meanwhile, the number of Americans who profess no religion is at an all-time high — and climbing. We are experiencing a revolution of irreligion.

If, as John Adams said, the U.S. Constitution was "made only for a moral and religious people" and is "wholly inadequate to the government of any other," where does that leave us?

Moreover, how do Catholics — that is, the moral and religious ones who are left — fit in to the American experiment?

The lay faithful are supposed to be more than mere citizens. The *Catechism of the Catholic Church* tells us that "intervening directly" in "political structuring and organization of social life" is our "vocation," and the U.S. bishops that "Jesus calls each of us to be a leaven in society," to "proclaim His message," and thereby influence the character of our nation.[8] How are we to fulfill that vocation, given the increasing stridency of American politics, the ongoing decline in the number of our coreligionists coupled with the waning influence of the Church in public life, and the living legacy of American anti-Catholicism?

---

[7] Gallup, "Church Attendance Has Declined in Most U.S. Religious Groups" (March 25, 2024), https://news.gallup.com/poll/642548/church-attendance-declined-religious-groups.aspx.

[8] *The Catechism of the Catholic Church* §2442; United States Catholic Conference, *Living the Gospel of Life: A Challenge to American Catholics* (1998) §7.

Three movements have proposed a way.

The first we may call the Benedict Option, based on Rod Dreher's eponymous 2017 bestseller. A powerful "liberal elite" has "revolutionized everything," Dreher writes in *The Benedict Option: A Strategy for Christians in a Post-Christian Nation*, and the American people, "either actively or passively, approve." In the culture war that began with the sexual revolution in the 1960s, Dreher says, conservative Christianity has been "routed," while secular nihilism has earned a resounding victory.

Full participation in mainstream society is, therefore, no longer possible for Catholics and other Christians who wish to "live a life of traditional virtue." Instead, Dreher says, we must "embrace exile from mainstream culture and construct a resilient counterculture." Rather than "wasting energy and resources fighting unwinnable political battles," the most effective way Christians can affect the organization of social life is to build "communities, institutions, and networks of resistance that can outwit, outlast, and eventually overcome the occupation" of America by the godless. Dreher calls the Benedict Option a "strategic withdrawal," a way for Christians to "pioneer" a way to live in faith-based oases of sanctity and stability — "Christian villages," he calls them — amid the "high tide of liquid modernity," as the culture corrodes around them.

That's one option. Another, likewise expressed in the title of a book, is regime change. Like Dreher, Patrick J. Deneen diagnoses a disease in these United States. The American regime, he posits, is "exhausted." Liberalism has failed, and the American embrace of economic and social "progress" has pitted "the few" against "the many," creating a tension that could result in either tyranny or civil war. The solution, Deneen argues in *Regime Change: Toward a Postliberal Future* (2023), is to replace the current ruling liberal elite with one aligned with "the wisdom of the people." This new elite would be formed by "a conservative ethos" and hold to "a common good conservatism." They would be "charged particularly as the trustees, defenders, and protectors of culture, tradition, and a longstanding way of life."

Regime change, in Deneen's imagining, would be a "peaceful but vigorous" overthrow of a "corrupt and corrupting liberal ruling class" and the creation of a "postliberal order." In a word, it would be a "rediscovery of early-modern forms of conservatism." The rulers of this postliberal order would "bolster populist political prospects as a working governmental and institutional force."

A third movement, called integralism, wouldn't merely replace the liberal ruling class with a conservative one; it would overhaul both our social organization and political structures. The proponents of integralism (who have journals and institutes at their command; it's not an insignificant movement) outdo Dreher and Deneen by calling for the construction of a ruling state based on Catholic values—an American theocracy, so to speak, in which Church and state are deeply intertwined, "everywhere and always together, bound together in the very unity of Christ," writes Andrew Willard Jones in *Before Church and State: A Study of Social Order in the Sacramental Kingdom of St. Louis IX* (2017). King Louis IX, Jones says, saw it as his duty to "build a society of virtue," and his regime aggressively enforced Catholic orthodoxy. Integralism is, at heart, the promotion of the ideal of a hierarchical society. Integralists would leverage the modern bureaucratic system to establish a state aligned with the Catholic conception of the common good. It is, however, far from a monolithic movement, and arguments about its implementation and overall implications are wide-ranging.

What all three movements share in common is the belief that Catholicism and Lockean liberalism (and its current iteration in a "woke" technocracy) are antithetical forces with competing conceptions of human nature and human flourishing. All three movements attempt to address—and alleviate—the deep fissures in the American body politic.

At this junction in our nation's history, all three are worthy of consideration. Moreover, the time is ripe to reconsider the very trajectory of our nation, and how — or if — Catholics fit into it. To that end, we asked thinkers of different stripes (and religious traditions) the following questions:

1. Is the American experiment an exhausted project?

2. In view of present and historic marginalization (coupled with a steady decline in the number of believers and institutional influence), can Catholics expect a "place at the table" of American politics?

3. Assuming authoritarian anti-Catholicism continues to gain ascendancy, what is the best way for Catholics to "intervene directly in the political structuring and organization of social life" in America? Is it in forming small "intentional communities" based on the Benedict Option? Is it in "regime change" in which a new elite reforms our present institutions? Is it in an "integralism" that overthrows them and replaces them with expressly Catholic institutions? Or is it in something else altogether?

4. Is there *any* hope for Catholics in American political life?

Respondents were given the choice to answer some or all the questions directly or to address the themes therein. Their replies originally appeared in a two-part symposium published in the *New Oxford Review*[9] and are here expanded, and their ideas elaborated. As this is a symposium, no attempt was made to achieve uniformity of response. Indeed, what follows is a lively variety of opinions and observations.

The options are set before us. Which shall we choose?

∞ ∞ ∞

PIETER VREE *is the editor of the* New Oxford Review, *a Catholic monthly magazine in its 48th year of continuous publication, and the father of six children.*

---

[9] "Symposium on Catholics & American Political Life," *New Oxford Review*, "Part I": Vol. XCI, Number 10 (Dec. 2024), pp. 16–34; "Part II," Vol. XCII, Number 1 (Jan.–Feb. 2025), pp. 20–34.

ACKNOWLEDGEMENTS

This book would not have been possible without the invaluable work of Barbara E. Rose, who helped prepare the "Symposium on Catholics & American Political Life" for publication in the *New Oxford Review*, or the input of John C. Médaille, who helped inspire it.

I

America is an Epic Comedy— We Just Caught the Bus in Time

VIRGINIA L. ARBERY

S THE AMERICAN EXPERIMENT AN exhausted project? I will begin to answer this question by describing comedy as did the late literary critic Louise Cowan, when she would distinguish it from tragedy for her students. In tragedy, the protagonist runs out of time to change the fatal choice he has made and misses the bus; in comedy, by contrast, the pedestrian, late and harried, running at full speed after the bus just as it begins to pull away, barely holding onto the bar to lift himself up the steps, manages to catch it. The word *exhaustion* suggests an expenditure of energy that has left one resourceless as the bus pulls away. If "the American experiment" refers to the American founding outlined by the proposed Philadelphia Constitution of 1787 and ratified in 1789, I answer "No," it is not exhausted: We have caught the bus.

The republican form, with prescribed powers enumerated at the national level and the residual powers left to the states, affording what Publius in the *Federalist Papers* called a "double security," and with a check on ambition through separation of powers, has not reached the point of exhaustion. To be sure, as Publius also writes, republican forms depend on a virtuous people more than any other form of rule. In *Federalist* 57 he writes:

> The aim of every political constitution is, or ought to be, first to obtain for rulers men who possess most wisdom to discern, and most virtue to pursue, the common good of the society, and in the

next place, to take the most effectual precautions
for keeping them virtuous while they continue to
hold their public trust.

Our founders achieved this aim; nevertheless, whether
the people remain faithful stewards of their legacy and
whether they choose men of virtue poses an enduring
challenge. The common good is dependent on men who
are guided by prudence and not by ideology. One must
admit that the people have not always chosen their rulers
accurately from among themselves. Often majorities have
been duped—but we have nevertheless caught the bus.

The miseducation of generations by those holding
philosophies which undermine republican liberty (Marxism,
socialism, progressivism) has contributed to the perception
that the American regime is "exhausted," or worse, a "project" flawed from its founding; so has the deliberate attack
on the *philosophia perennis* on which liberty depends. One
might also argue, as did 20th-century political philosopher
Willmoore Kendall, that a "derailment" began with the
emphasis on equality instead of on liberty pronounced
in Lincoln's "Gettysburg Address," which, I would add,
resulted in unintended consequences. But neither this
miseducation nor the impetus toward equality were inevitable; neither was the decline in virtue accompanying
these two movements.

For generations, "prestigious" schools undermined
attachment to the regime and its classical roots. Secondary
schools and grammar schools followed the lead. Critical race
theory and the 1619 Project added to the Marxist indoc-
trination begun by Charles Beard's *An Economic Interpretation of the Constitution of the United States of America*
(1913), which taught students to dismiss their country as
undemocratic and oligarchic. Providentially, COVID-19
revealed to the generality the DEI agenda of school boards
that mandated perverse reading material while rearranging
sexually segregated bathrooms, meanwhile teaching deeply
biased historical accounts as facts in the classroom. COVID

lockdowns and mandates also revealed how passive and submissive Americans had become when denied their most fundamental rights, such as the freedom of religion.

The second Trump administration's appeal to the common sense and decency of the American people has begun a counterrevolution; citizens recognize that the progressivist revolution disenfranchised them and attempted to overturn nature herself. Language, which had undergone a sea change, is being restored to its obvious meanings. Almost overnight, girls are girls, and boys are boys again. The usurpers' distrust of the American people and their misplaced trust in experts replaced the Constitution with the administrative state. This unfounded fourth branch undermined both the aims and the governmental structure of the Constitution. Unaccountable bureaucrats nearly displaced the two deliberative elected bodies. Federal courts assumed the legislative function improperly. In addition, and perhaps worst of all, progressivism enervated public spiritedness and civic engagement.

But the fiber of attentive citizenship is more resilient than critics of our regime have supposed. We still witness — do we not? — effective officeholders who take seriously their constitutional duties. A Supreme Court refreshed with judges who answer to the Constitution, and a Congress revived by members who resist usurpations of other branches, prove the durability of "ambition counteracting ambition" (*Federalist* 51). Attentive citizens awakened to see the unfolding of "the violence of majority faction," which the founders feared might happen. The founders saw the antidote to majority faction in the "large extended republic" comprised of states with diverse populations of different talents and faculties of acquiring property and with different religions.

Though some of my fellow Catholics see this last point as a cause for dismay, Alexis de Tocqueville identified freedom of religion nearly two hundred years ago as a strength unique to America. When political power resides in the

Church, he argued, believers grow deeply disillusioned by the this-worldly concerns and secular choices of their spiritual authorities. The "spirit of religion," first brought to these shores by our Puritan forebears, flourishes when the "spirit of liberty" allows variety. Though the visiting Frenchman did not do so, American Catholics have (often ungraciously) dismissed the role of our Puritan forebears whose "spirit of freedom" emitted a "biblical perfume." Orestes Brownson, the great Catholic convert of the nineteenth century, argued of the Puritans that "Never were men more serious, more deeply in earnest; and it was in obedience to what they held to be the voice of God that they preached, fasted, sung psalms, prayed.... They would have organized and maintained society, except in not enjoying celibacy, after the mode of a Catholic monastery."[1] American Catholics should widen their hearts and celebrate the anti-Catholic Puritans who lay the foundation for limited government by rooting it in the ultimate authority of God, from whom all political authority derives.

George Washington pronounced that "religion and morality" are the "indispensable supports" upon which our liberties and civic virtues depend. As de Tocqueville observed, the American's ready inclination to associate for commonly held aims is one of the bulwarks against the leveling tendency of equality. There are many signs that we have caught the bus. Parents, likeminded believers, and Catholic intellectuals and businessmen have formed associations to resist policies adverse to the common good. Many fine classical schools have been founded in the past forty years, and the number of charter schools and homeschooling associations is truly heartening. The Institute for Catholic Liberal Education, for one, seeks to guide diocesan schools to adopt classically oriented curricula.

Liberty is harder to achieve and to keep, de Tocqueville wrote, while equality's "charms" gratify citizens daily. But

---

[1] *The Works of Orestes A. Brownson*, Collected and Arranged by Henry F. Browson (Detroit, MI: Thorndike Nourse, 1882).

many religious and political associations, such as right-to-life committees and think tanks (the Heritage Foundation, the American Enterprise Institute, and the Claremont Institute, among others) demonstrate that citizens, their liberty under duress, believe that their efforts can be efficacious. These and smaller groups, including one aimed solely at preserving the electoral college, indicate that perseverance and encouragement under the current administration will re-invigorate constitutionalism and civic virtue.

And perhaps we might extend de Tocqueville's astute observations to other political and social aspects of our own day. Having a "place at the table" suggests that we must break bread with our neighbors, not lord it over them. American political life has likely never seen such energetic Catholic officeholders at both the federal and state level. To the extent that governors like Ron DeSantis and Greg Abbott, judges like Clarence Thomas and Amy Comey Barrett, and Catholic congressmen (almost a third of the body) are faithful constitutionalists, our future as Catholic citizens is a call to hospitality. We are Americans, and those who would build irreconcilable barriers between faith and patriotism display not their orthodoxy but an egregious ingratitude. At the very least, they evince their lack of the political virtue of prudence. If we refuse to honor the continuum between the legacy of Christendom and that of republican liberty, we Catholics could, in fact, lose our "place at the table."

Let us, in short, celebrate the energized prospects for Catholic political participation. The reaction to Kamala Harris and Tim Walz's anti-Catholic sentiments and policies continues to be lively. No law prohibits Catholics from entering politics locally or nationally. In fact, in running for the local school board last year, I learned that non-Catholics are grateful to be able to vote for someone who can articulate traditional principles and practices. I found that restoring the centrality of the word *nature* resonated with my neighbors. However, my fellow older Catholics in the town (outside those who teach at my college) tend to be less traditional even than many non-Catholics. Their sense of compassion often gets in the way of their good sense. Well-educated younger Catholics should take the lead in government at every level, as the young William F. Buckley and James Buckley did in their day.

Though I deeply appreciate my friend Rod Dreher's nuanced presentation of the Benedict Option, and though I tend to admire purists and idealists such as "integralism" attracts, neither can widen the participation in government upon which the fuller restoration of public virtue and constitutionalism depends. Indeed, I believe that small intentional communities make a significant difference in forming future citizens who can lead through both example and competency, and paired with educational reform, those involved in public service must be content with playing the "long game."

I am not naïve; not every ethical issue will be addressed. Nevertheless, my shared impatience over the continued slaughter of the unborn, my dismay over Trump's hardhat approach to Ukraine and outreach to Putin, my sorrow over his endorsement of IVF — all these policies and others — do not lead me to pout in a corner with other malcontents.

Finally, I am heartily opposed to "regime change." I disagree with Patrick Deneen and others who argue that the American founding was flawed. I concur with Robert Reilly, Daniel J. Mahoney, Paul DeHart, and others who admire and appreciate our political roots, regarding them as harmonious with the natural law. Pursuing isolated Protestant or Catholic communities will fail to keep the principles and beliefs we hold dear in front of the public mind. We should cherish our small, highly faithful communities and institutions (such as Wyoming Catholic College), but we must do so while engaging those outside of them.

To preserve hope, we should return to our sources. Fortunately, our pre-founding roots are not in the Enlightenment but in traditional Aristotelian and Thomistic thought. Recalling John Winthrop's definition of liberty would be one excellent place to begin:

> There is a Liberty of Corrupt Nature, which is affected both by Men and Beasts, to do what they list, and this Liberty is inconsistent with Authority, . . . and all the Ordinances of God are bent against it. But there is a Civil, a Moral, a Federal Liberty, which is the proper End and Object of Authority; it is a Liberty for that only which is just and good; for Liberty you are to stand with the hazard of your Lives.

We must hazard our very lives to stay on that bus.

∞ ∞ ∞

VIRGINIA L. ARBERY, *Ph.D., is an associate professor of humanities at Wyoming Catholic College in Lander, Wyoming.*

2

A Less Prominent Place, Perhaps, but Still a Place from which to Serve

CASEY CHALK

CROSS TWO MILLENNIA, CATHO-lics have participated in a remarkable variety of political arrangements—some hospitable to the Church, others openly hostile. There were converts among the patrician families of the pagan Roman imperium. In medieval Europe, the Church enjoyed a pride of place, anointing kings and influencing governing decisions (and, inversely, suffering those rulers' meddling in ecclesial affairs). More recently, Catholics have taken to liberal democracy, sometimes forming (or dominating) political parties that led ruling coalitions, such as the Christian Democrats in Germany and Italy, the Popular Republican Movement in France, and Fianna Fáil in Ireland. This has been the case even in countries where Catholics are a small minority. Predominantly Shinto Japan has had no fewer than *three* Catholic prime ministers. As of December 2024, Catholic politicians were serving in the legislatures of Hindu-majority India, Muslim-majority Indonesia, and Buddhist- and Taoist-majority Taiwan. Of course, Catholic participation in the *polis* does not mean the faithful aren't often engaged in a delicate and tense game in which they must navigate (often competing) allegiances to both Church and state. This was true even in the medieval French kingdom of St. Louis IX—which integralists and postliberals present as the apotheosis of collaborative Church-state relations—given the inevitable competition between these two sources of power. The Investiture Controversy, the martyrdom of St. Thomas Becket, and the Hundred Years' War, among many other examples, demonstrate that medieval European Catholicism, whatever its many virtues, was a contentious, confused, and violent period of Church history. It was, after all, *an ecclesial court* that convicted St. Joan of Arc of heresy and permitted her burning at the stake.

As far as I know, no Catholics have been executed for practicing the faith here in America. That is not to downplay the very real persecution Catholics have faced in recent days — witness the crackdown on pro-life Catholic activists by the U.S. Department of Justice, or the FBI analysis on "radical traditionalist Catholics."[1] In February 2025 two legislative committees in the State of Washington advanced two bills intended to force priests to violate the seal of Confession.[2] But we should keep things in perspective. Approximately one in seven American patients receive medical care in a Catholic hospital. About 1.7 million American kids are educated in Catholic schools. Catholics comprise twenty-eight percent of Congress, a percentage greater than that of self-identifying Catholics in the general population. Our nation has more Catholic media outlets and publishing houses than any other country in the world, exceeding those of even predominantly Catholic nations with far higher rates of Mass attendance.

Granted, a growing number of Americans don't like this. They don't want Americans going to Catholic hospitals that regulate care related to pregnancy, gender confusion, or pending death.[3] They don't want children educated with

---

[1] Joe Bukuras, "Acquitted pro-life activist Mark Houck reveals details of 'reckless' FBI raid; will press charges," *Catholic News Agency* (Feb. 1, 2023), https://www.catholicnewsagency.com/news/253523/acquitted-pro-life-activist-mark-houck-reveals-details-of-fbi-raid-will-press-charges; The Federal Bureau of Investigation, "Radical Traditionalist Catholic Ideology Part 01," https://vault.fbi.gov/radical-traditionalist-catholic-ideology/radical-traditionalist-catholic-ideology-part-01/view.

[2] McKenna Snow, "Washington state committees advance legislation trying to force priests to violate seal of Confession," *Catholic Vote* (Feb. 12, 2025), https://catholicvote.org/washington-state-committees-advance-legislation-trying-to-force-priests-to-violate-seal-of-confession.

[3] Frances Stead Sellers and Meena Venkataramanan, "Spread of Catholic

curricula that oppose the dogmas of the sexual revolution or critical race theory.[4] And they don't want Catholic media to be free to publish material that reflects magisterial teaching, which they deem disinformation.[5]

Despite her obvious strengths, it is undeniable that the Church's cultural and political capital is eroding. Though as of February 2025 Mass attendance rates had finally returned to pre-pandemic levels, our nation is undergoing a seismic shift in religious observance among younger generations. As sociologist Stephen Bullivant has cataloged,[6] the proportion of U.S. adults under the age of thirty with no religious affiliation jumped from ten percent in 1972 to thirty-four percent in 2018. And of the approximately forty-one million "nonverts," the term for those who grew up in a religious tradition but are now religious unaffiliated, sixteen million of them are former Catholics. On top of that, since 1988, the Catholic Church in the United States has lost about two thousand parishes, due either to closings or mergers.[7] This will all affect the Church's ability to influence American society. Some observers have interpreted the declining religiosity of American Catholics — and American Christians more broadly — as evidence that the American founding as a political experiment is inherently flawed. Catholic convert L. Brent Bozell II, writing in 1968

hospitals limits reproductive care across the U.S." *The Washington Post* (Oct. 10, 2022), https://www.washingtonpost.com/health/2022/10/10/abortion-catholic-hospitals-birth-control.

[4] Anna Sugg, "I'm a student in Catholic school. It isn't a safe place for my LGBTQ+ classmates," *Courier Journal* (March 22, 2023), https://www.courier-journal.com/story/opinion/2023/03/22/im-a-student-in-catholic-school-its-not-safe-for-lgbtq-classmates/70029038007.

[5] Eric Sammons, "My Catholic Beliefs Landed Me in Twitter Jail," *Crisis Magazine* (Jan. 20, 2021), https://crisismagazine.com/opinion/my-catholic-beliefs-landed-me-in-twitter-jail.

[6] Stephen Bullivant, *Nonverts: The Making of Ex-Christian America* (New York: Oxford University Press, 2022).

[7] Michael Lipka, Pew Research Center, "The number of U.S. Catholics has grown, so why are there fewer parishes?" (Nov. 6, 2014), https://www.pewresearch.org/short-reads/2014/11/06/the-number-of-u-s-catholics-has-grown-so-why-are-there-fewer-parishes.

for his Catholic magazine *Triumph*, argued that it was impossible to reconcile the Declaration of Independence and its claim that governments derive "their just powers from the governed" with Pope Leo XIII's assertion in *Immortale dei* that "all power must proceed from God." Thus, Bozell claimed, "the Constitution has not only failed; it was bound to fail."[8]

This thinking is increasingly popular among politically conservative, traditionalist Catholics who typically describe themselves as either postliberals or integralists. *New Polity*, a popular forum for Catholic postliberal thought, publishes content labeling as anti-Christian such manifestations of liberal modernity as police forces, capitalism, and the stock market.[9] Postliberal Catholic thinker D.C. Schindler argues that America's founding was so deeply influenced by flawed Lockean thinking about human flourishing and freedom that our nation's entire system of government is diabolical, meaning it is a deceptive, soulless, and self-destructive substitution of reality. In its prioritization of the private will of individuals and dissociation of freedom from the good, the American political experiment, claims Schindler, is antithetical to both classical and Christian understandings of man, his relationship to the *polis*, and his natural and supernatural ends.

I would counter that many principles of the American founding are also visible in that Catholic tradition. The idea of a regime defined by consent of the governed, for example, is as ancient as Cicero and can be found in the medieval and early modern world, such as in the Magna

---

[8] L. Brent Bozell, II, "The Death of the Constitution," *The Best of Triumph* (Front Royal, VA: Christendom Press, 2001), pp. 388–391.
[9] Marc Barnes, "The Christian Abolition of the Police," *New Polity* (June 13, 2020), https://newpolity.com/blog/the-christian-abolition-of-the-official-police; Andrew Willard Jones, "Capitalism Produces Socialism"; *New Polity*, Issue 2.4 (Fall 2021), https://newpolity.com/blog/capitalism-produces-socialism; Jacob Imam, Marc Barnes, "Should Christians Invest in the Stockmarket," *New Polity*, Issue 4.1 (Winter 2022), https://newpolity.com/blog/should-christians-invest-in-the-stockmarket.

Carta and the writings of Duns Scotus, Nicholas of Cusa, Thomas Aquinas, and Thomas More.[10] Even Dante makes an argument for the separation of Church and state in the *Divine Comedy*.[11] Augustine hints at natural rights in *City of God*.[12] The concept also appears in canon law in the Middle Ages and the Renaissance-era School of Salamanca, which argued in favor of individuals asserting their natural rights against the collective. As Catholic academic Matthew Mehan has noted, *pace* errant popular portrayals, Thomas More defended both religious toleration and freedom of speech.[13]

Moreover, whatever John Locke's influence over the framers of the Constitution, he did not found our American republic. Academics are inclined to view things almost exclusively through the prism of ideas: this individual influenced this individual who influenced that individual, and that explains [fill in the blank] modern phenomena. Though that analysis can be illuminating, it can also be simplistic, especially when we are talking about politics, which is defined at least as much, if not more so, by the practicalities of constituencies, external threats, and budgets than it is by the theories of political philosophers. Politics is about making prudential judgments in a complicated world of competing interests, where achieving principle-based objectives often involves compromise, even, to some degree, of those very principles. The founders confronted precisely these complexities when they formed our republic.

As many scholars have argued, the framers of our Constitution had a strong sense of the natural law, the importance of organized (Christian) religion, and that man's happiness would be found naturally in virtue and supernaturally in God. It's true that, apart from Charles Carroll, Daniel Carroll, and Thomas Fitzsimons, they were not Catholic. But if

---

[10] Thomas Aquinas, *Summa Theologiae*, I-II, q. 105, art. 1.
[11] Dante, *Purgatorio* 15 and 16.
[12] Augustine, *City of God*, Book XIX.
[13] Matthew Mehan, "A Memento Mori for Today: Lessons from Thomas More," *Public Discourse* (July 5, 2018), https://www.thepublicdiscourse.com/2018/07/22101.

the complaint is that the founding was not sufficiently Catholic, we should consider other, majority-Catholic nations who have affirmed Catholic teaching in their founding documents. The 1937 constitution of the Republic of Ireland, for example, was not only explicitly Trinitarian but acknowledged the Catholic Church's "special position" as the guardian of the faith of most citizens and referred to her as "the Church of Christ." Those references were removed in the 1970s. In the Ireland of today, abortion and same-sex marriage are legal, and weekly Mass attendance dropped from ninety-one percent in 1975 to twenty-seven percent in 2024, comparable to rates in the United States.

However much we may mourn the declining influence of Catholicism in America, Catholics still possess cultural and political capital. *Roe v. Wade* currently lies defeated by a majority-Catholic Supreme Court. However cynical we may be about contemporary politics, Catholic elected officials still promote ways of life that align with the Catholic conception of human dignity at the local, state, and national levels. Practicing Catholic J. D. Vance less than two weeks into his term as vice president evoked the Catholic concept of *ordo amoris*, the "order of charity," in a discussion on immigration. Two weeks later, he excoriated a room full of European politicians and bureaucrats for attacking religious liberty, ending his speech by quoting Pope St. John Paul II. To forfeit such positive momentum, whether because we have often been losing or because of some perceived defect in the American founding, seems naïve and irresponsible. It would be naïve because it implies that we will be safe in our retreat to Steubenville, Front Royal, Naples, or one of the other bastions of traditional Catholicism. If our enemies are as anti-Catholic as we perceive them to be, do we really think they'll disregard our little Catholic enclaves? Imagine, instead, innumerable media exposés of our "patriarchal" or "bigoted" communities for alleged misogynist or transphobic discrimination, which in turn provoke federal investigations and prosecutions. A withdrawal would be irresponsible because it would mean leaving to the wolves millions of our fellow citizens, Catholic or not, who would thus be susceptible to policies and propaganda that would harm their bodies and their souls. Such thinking is antithetical to the heroism of, say, St. Elizabeth of Portugal, who helped facilitate treaties between Iberian kingdoms and prevented a civil war, or St. Peter Claver, who ministered to hundreds of thousands of slaves in the New Kingdom of Granada (present-day Colombia).

Each Catholic's response to the Church's loss of influence requires prudential thinking. For some, keeping the faith may mean moving from one place to another because of state policies that inhibit religious practice. For others, it may mean rising to combat evil by leveraging all the professional or political weapons at their disposal. For still others, it may mean continuing to quietly, faithfully fulfill their vocation in places progressively more hostile to the Catholic way of life.

The American experiment is not exhausted, not as long as Catholics are permitted to participate in the current regime, warts and all. The testimony of Catholics over many centuries in many political scenarios should give us hope and caution us against doomsday thinking. Our place at the table may sometimes be less prominent, but it is a place from which we may still yet save lives and souls — and, I pray, make a few saints in the process. As Our Lord said when confronted with political threats far greater than our own: "Now is my soul troubled. And what shall I say? 'Father, save me from this hour'? No, for this purpose I have come to this hour" (John 12:27).

∞ ∞ ∞

CASEY CHALK *is a contributing editor of the* New Oxford Review *and senior contributor at* The Federalist. *His latest book is* The Obscurity of Scripture: Disputing Sola Scriptura and the Protestant Notion of Biblical Perspicuity *(Emmaus Road Publishing).*

3

"Stuck Inside of Mobile With the Memphis Blues Again"

WILL HOYT

HERE ARE TIMES IN ALL CULTURES when the fairy tale about the king not wearing clothes becomes relevant, and all it takes is a simple nudge for people to wake up and finally see an obvious and extremely important fact that, only moments before, had not been visible. Such is our time, now, in America.

Take the set of questions motivating this symposium.

First question: "Is the American experiment exhausted?" Answer: No. Given that the American experiment, so called, is the place where Western Civilization is actively on trial with the entire world watching from the balcony, as it were, our experiment in self-governance can hardly be said to be exhausted.

Second question: "Can Catholics realistically expect a 'place at the table' of American politics?" Answer: Of course. Indeed, you could make a persuasive case that, ever since the election of John F. Kennedy, Catholics have created the playing field on which political life happens, let alone driven discussions proper. Moreover, even if Catholics hadn't done this, we have been able, all along, to exercise the same voting privileges that every other citizen has and will continue to have, barring invasion by another country or civilizational collapse.

Third question: "Assuming authoritarian anti-Catholicism keeps gaining ascendancy," is the best option for Catholics to form "small, local, intentional communities based on the Benedict Option," or commit to "regime change" by reconfiguring the administrative state so that social life in this country conforms better to Catholic social teaching? Answer: No. Outside of pedigreed monastic orders, intentional communities always fail, and, as for reconfiguring the administrative state, that project would, perforce, rely on Herbert Marcuse's concept of repressive tolerance to the same degree that New Left projects do.

Fourth question: "Assuming authoritarian anti-Catholicism keeps gaining ascendancy," are there any other options besides regime change for "intervening directly in the political structuring and organization of social life in America?" (This is the key question, the kicker.) Answer: Yes! It is to defend the written charter otherwise known as the U.S. Constitution and recognize it as the miraculously apropos instrument that it is.

Let me explain.

Extreme polarization invites handwringing. Like Bob Dylan fifty years ago, we've all been thinking *Aw, Mama, can this really be the end?* But it's not the end. Sure, the West as on view in Virgil may be over. But that doesn't mean some other form of civilization won't replace it. As Dylan knew, and we now also know, we've simply been stuck in Mobile with the Memphis blues again and can, therefore, kick up our heels owing to newly arrived empirical evidence that woke thinking combined with belief in the rightness of lecturing presumably unenlightened provincials is itself a religion with its own sacraments, the most sacred of which is to never question whether common sense might mean something held in common rather than something owned by commoners. Other important sacraments in this new religion are categorical refusals to see what is right before one's eyes, and, of course, wearing a *keffiyeh*.

Thanks to evidence like this, we can all of us finally see that the problematic (not premodern) aspects of liberalism — namely, that an ontological zone called neutrality exists and, no less importantly, that reason can exist apart from faith — are completely baseless. And that fact, in turn, means we are freed — you might say liberated — to pose the one question we've been needing to ask all along so as to effectively meet postmodern challenges by asking ourselves which faith among the many faiths comprising our new confirmedly multicultural society most effectively enables glimpses of the good, the true, and the beautiful.

But let us pinch ourselves to make sure we are awake and not dreaming as we finally grasp that we are standing on the threshold of a beginning rather than an end and call to mind John Rawls' groundbreaking apologia for liberalism, *A Theory of Justice*, published some fifty-three years ago when I last attended school.

I admired Rawls then because he had the inner strength to hold ground as an infantryman in New Guinea and the Philippines during the Second World War, and I continue to admire the man owing to the elegance of his arguments. The beauty of Rawls' approach is that he sets up his arguments as thought experiments in which consensus emerges amongst interested parties regarding which set of rules would be needed for a society to be practically just. Rawls calls his goal "justice as fairness," and his signature move in both *A Theory of Justice* and *Political Liberalism* (1993), is to ask readers to imagine that the parties in his thought experiments deliberate behind a "veil" of ignorance regarding which position they will eventually hold in the society they will occupy once the thought experiment ends, and depend only on "public reason" when designing a polity in which a variety of faith communities have a stake. During the 1970s, and even during the 1990s, Rawls' arguments were provocative in the best sense and therefore helpful. Now, however, they seem off-target and, to that extent, worthless. Why? Simple. There is more at stake now. Bona-fide cultural life is itself on the line, given that half the country is starting to think of religion as ideology; hence, the crucial question is no longer how to ensure distributive justice. Instead, it is which faith, which kind of liturgically based rationality, we should commit to as a place in which to think and from which to act.

Alasdair MacIntyre is deservedly famous for *After Virtue*

(1981), the book in which he rather spectacularly critiqued "emotivism" by likening its arrival in moral philosophy to a bomb's and then surveying the wreckage. Moreover, his conclusion that we are waiting for a new, "undoubtedly very different" St. Benedict is as stirring today as it was in 1981. Therefore, it makes sense that Rod Dreher, for example, would want to salute *After Virtue* by naming his book about intentional communities *The Benedict Option*. But *After Virtue* is not MacIntyre's best book. The book for which he will be remembered is a compilation of Gifford Lectures delivered in Edinburgh, Scotland, called *Three Rival Versions of Moral Inquiry* (1988), in which he explains three things: first, that our current postmodern predicament derives from the mistaken assumption that (owing to the failure of the Enlightenment-based belief that universals can only be glimpsed outside of particular historical determinants) those same universals don't exist; second, that perennial philosophy's incarnational basis — that is to say, its faith-based assumption that universals come into view *through* historical determinants rather than in spite of them — is the perfect, tailor-made solution to that same predicament; and, third, that the only way forward is to ask which historically determined school of thought best favors a just and humane world. "Encyclopaedic" (Enlightenment-based)? "Genealogical" (Nietzchean)? Or "Tradition-Dependent" (Thomistic)?

It used to be hard even to get people to think of asking this question. But now we're all asking it, and thanks to the electoral college and rights enumerated in a First Amendment that descends all the way from the Magna Carta, we should be able to keep asking it and in that way activate the only truly common good this side of Heaven.

∞ ∞ ∞

WILL HOYT *is the author of* The Seven Ranges: Ground Zero for the Staging of America *(Front Porch Republic Books, 2021) and a contributing editor of the* New Oxford Review. *A former carpenter, he now manages an inn for oil and gas workers near Wheeling, West Virginia.*

4

A Permanent Seat on the Right Side of the Table

GEORGE HAWLEY

S AN EVANGELICAL CHRISTIAN and a political conservative, I share many of the concerns of orthodox Catholics about the direction of American politics and culture. I am allergic to doomsaying, however, and I urge Christians of all traditions not to despair or assume only radical changes can set our country back on track. We have a great amount of work ahead of us, but Christianity historically has thrived in the United States within a classical liberal framework, and it would be a mistake to abandon that tradition.

I urge Catholics to note the positive developments in American politics over the past century. Although Christianity seems to be declining as a cultural force, and an alarming percentage of Americans now answer "none" when asked their religious identity, there is arguably less anti-Catholic animus in this country than ever before. A majority of the U.S. Supreme Court is Catholic, including most of the justices who voted to overturn *Roe*. Former House Speaker Nancy Pelosi is also Catholic, as is former President Joe Biden. Vice President J.D. Vance is a Catholic convert. When considered in the context of America's history of anti-Catholic bigotry, it is remarkable how little attention these facts receive.

I understand that many orthodox Catholics are discouraged that leading Catholic Democrats choose not to promote Church doctrine when it comes to public policy, especially as it relates to abortion. Nonetheless, we have come a long way since 1960, when John F. Kennedy had to convince a skeptical nation that his Catholicism should not disqualify him for the presidency. In 1928, Al Smith's Catholic faith played a role in his humiliating defeat in his race against Herbert Hoover. Joe Biden wasn't hamstrung in such a way. Catholic identity is no longer a hindrance to achieving political power in the United States. This is worth celebrating.

Catholics have played an especially underappreciated role in shaping the American Right and, by extension, the Republican Party. For much of our nation's history, political conservatism was associated with anti-Catholicism. The Know-Nothing Movement of the mid-1800s was overtly anti-Catholic, as was the Ku Klux Klan in the early twentieth century. But the postwar conservative movement ended this tradition. Among the intellectuals and journalists who set the American Center Right's agenda, Catholics were massively overrepresented. This was especially true at *National Review*, the flagship journal of American conservatism. William F. Buckley, Russell Kirk, Willmoore Kendall, L. Brent Bozell II, Frank Meyer, Thomas Molnar, and James Burnham were all either raised Catholic or converted as adults — though, admittedly, in the case of Meyer and Burnham, they waited until they were literally on their deathbeds to do so.

Sen. Barry Goldwater, the first postwar presidential nominee to embrace the conservative movement, chose Rep. William Miller, a Catholic, as his running mate. That ticket was defeated in a landslide, but Catholics played an outsized role in growing conservatism as a powerful force in the coming decades, setting the stage for Ronald Reagan's electoral landslides. Paul Weyrich and Phyllis Schlafly, the most effective conservative activists and organizers in the twentieth century, were devout Catholics. They played a key role in creating an ecumenical movement of cultural conservatives that transcended religious sectarianism.

If we ever witness an authoritarian anti-Catholic turn in the United States, we can be fully confident it will not come from the mainstream political Right, thanks largely to the Catholics who built and worked within conservative institutions. Catholics will have a seat on the right side of the nation's ideological table for the foreseeable future. This is no small accomplishment.

I understand the impulse to withdraw from mainstream politics, especially at a time when cultural trends are pulling the nation in a more secular direction. I endorse efforts by Christians — Catholic and Protestant — to build strong, intentional Christian communities. I am more skeptical about efforts to change the nation's trajectory via partisan politics or revolution. The quixotic pursuit of Christian nationalism — be it Protestant dominionism, Catholic integralism, or some other variety — will almost certainly be self-defeating.

Conservative Catholics with theocratic inclinations should be aware that they are not the first Americans to pursue that path, and the historical record will not inspire their confidence. Bozell, Goldwater's ghostwriter and a close collaborator with Buckley, eventually broke with the conservative movement, launching the magazine *Triumph* in 1966. He hoped to import something akin to Francisco Franco's variety of pro-Catholic authoritarianism to the United States. Few people remember this, as the effort was an abysmal failure, and the magazine ceased publication after a decade. What reason do we have for believing a similar effort will be more successful now? If anything, the public is less amenable to these kinds of arguments than it was five decades ago. Furthermore, we can question the efficacy of expressly pro-Catholic governments, even when they succeed in taking power. For all the superficial Catholic piety of Franco's Spain or Salazar's Portugal, people quickly moved away from the Church as soon as the state took its thumb off the scale. Both countries are now much less religiously observant than is the United States.

I am not unsympathetic to the impulse to withdraw from the mainstream political and cultural arena. One could reasonably argue that the upward mobility and cultural assimilation of Catholics into American life came at a cost. As historian Patrick Allitt noted in his book *Catholic Intellectuals and Conservative Politics in America, 1950–1985,* "To be a Catholic in the 1950s was to be aware of oneself as a member of a minority group, set apart from the rest of society by a pattern of beliefs, ritual actions, liturgical practices, food taboos, and even a distinctive view of the nation's history and Western Civilization." As Allitt persuasively argued, however, by the 1970s, that distinctiveness had faded. Today, it seems to have disappeared entirely. I will not tell Catholics how they should feel about this, but I can understand why some orthodox Catholics feel what historian Philip Gleason called the "crisis of Americanization." I nonetheless urge Catholics not to lose sight of what they gained during this era.

As a conservative with many concerns about ongoing trends in the United States, I hope to see Christians of all varieties actively engaged in every element of public life, balancing the desire for a healthy, pro-family culture with a tolerance for cultural differences and religious pluralism, maintaining respect for the institutions that have long served our country well. That engagement of course includes politics, but we also need a renewed focus on art and education, at both the local and national level. I hope Catholics will remain an important part of mainstream American life, rather than withdrawing to quietism or embracing theocratic flights of fancy.

I am not downplaying the many theological, cultural, and sometimes political differences between Catholics and Protestants — or, for that matter, among Protestants. These are real, and there are certain issues over which we are simply at an impasse. I nonetheless increasingly agree with Tocqueville's assessment that "all sects in the United States are reunited in the great Christian community, and the morality of Christianity is everywhere the same."

Previous generations of Catholics fought hard to gain tolerance and, eventually, respect and significant influence in American life. They still possess these things, even as the country is becoming less Christian. As America increasingly realized the ideal of religious liberty, Catholics were some of the main beneficiaries. A problem with that liberty, of course, is that many people will turn their backs on God. The good news is that recent polling data indicates that secularization has plateaued, and catastrophic religious decline in America no longer appears inevitable. This does not make our many challenges less real, but despair is both unwarranted and contrary to the belief in God's goodness and justice. Regardless of our challenges, it would be a mistake to trust state power to reverse our current course.

∞ ∞ ∞

GEORGE HAWLEY *is associate professor of political science at the University of Alabama. He is the author of eight books, including* Right-Wing Critics of American Conservatism, Conservatism in a Divided America *and* The Moderate Majority: Real GOP Voters and the Myth of Mass Republican Radicalization.

5

Strike the Shepherd and the Sheep Will Be Scattered

KAN ITO

S THERE ANY HOPE FOR CATHO-
lics in American political life? Yes! Let me explain.
I am not a Catholic. I do not hold to any particular religious creed. However, I believe there is something
greater than us, some transcendence that made the universe
and informs our consciences. Call me a Kantian, if you
like, or perhaps a neo-Platonist. Whatever the appellation,
I am convinced there is a transcendental moral law, and
we ignore it at the peril of our values and souls.

In my forty-plus years in the United States, during which
time I have been both an observer of and a participant
in Washington politics, I have seen what happens when
the moral law is scorned. Not just in Washington, but
in America at large. And not just in America, but in my
home country of Japan, too. In Japan, Buddhist monks
traditionally have taught morals to the people, instilling in
congregations a sense of right and wrong. In the United
States, pastors and priests, brothers and nuns have done
this. In both countries, the people have grown indifferent
to the voices of moral awareness and the deeper meaning
of life. The results are as we see today: Both countries
have become morally apathetic. The rich profit off the
destruction of nations, the elites are materialistic and shal-
low minded, and the poor are ground down deeper into
despair and powerlessness.

Since the Cold War, the U.S. government has relied
on raw military power to keep unipolar world order
and has aggressively tried to strengthen U.S. global

hegemony—without meaningful consent from ordinary American people. This imperium is waning, and American society seems to be falling apart. The list of things that dismay Catholics is probably similar to the list of things that dismay me: drug addiction, homelessness, artificially exaggerated LGBTQ issues, the loss of childhood innocence, violence in the streets, and the chaos of unregulated immigration and the ensuing destruction of national coherence. No amount of political or economic power can cure these ills, because they are, at root, spiritual-philosophical-moral issues. Without shepherds to guide and feed the flock, the flock descends into anarchy and ruin. Without Christian (or classical humanist) morality, American society loses its coherence and integrity. We are seeing it happen right in front of our eyes.

Some American politicians and thinkers, including prominent ones, have called to make America a Catholic nation. I agree with them. American politics cannot be guided wisely without a religious (or philosophical) people, and the Catholic Church is able to make the greatest contribution to this restoration effort. Though I am not Catholic, I honestly believe the Catholic Church has the greatest potential to restore sanity to the troubled nation. After all, it was the Catholic Church that stubbornly defended civilization and probity amid the collapse of the Roman imperium.

∞ ∞ ∞

KAN ITO *is a foreign-policy analyst working in Washington, D.C., and Tokyo. He is the author of five books on international politics, European diplomatic history, and Chinese military policy.*

6

Zoomer Catholics:
A Hopeful Sign, a Future Aborning

A. JAMES MCADAMS

MERICAN CATHOLICS HAVE REA-
son to worry that some people would happily rel-
egate them permanently to the political and social
sidelines. When they decry the secularizing forces that have
undermined traditional religious institutions and values,
they are ridiculed by self-proclaimed public intellectuals,
talk-show hosts, and opportunistic politicians who treat
them as if they were unreflective Neanderthals. However,
as Casey Chalk has pointed out in his contribution to this
volume, it is a stretch to argue that Catholics are completely
marginalized in a country where they occupy powerful posi-
tions throughout the judicial system, educate millions of ele-
mentary and high school students, and boast a sizable media
presence. Nevertheless, for the purpose of argument, let us
assume that American Catholicism really is at death's door.
What remedies do orthodox Catholics offer to restore the
Church's authority and infuse her with a renewed vitality?

Among the three solutions Pieter Vree has described
in the introduction to this volume, Rod Dreher's idea
of building heroic networks of resistance to propagate a
resilient counterculture seems quaintly old-fashioned. It is
an example of a recurring romantic motif in the American
story. For my generation, the quest for an alternative realm
of moral solidarity was epitomized by the hippie communes
of the late 1960s. Thousands of disaffected young people
went down to the countryside, where they hoped to cultivate
peace and love. Instead, they discovered that they could not
even grow turnips, let alone overcome their many differences.

Similarly, the integralists' dream of infusing the established political order with Catholic conceptions of family values, justice, and authority may appeal to some of us. Yet it only passes muster if we ignore the fact that the U.S. is home to multiple non-Christian religious traditions. Moreover, Christians of all shades and types have vastly different understandings of these values, some of which are tinged with anti-Catholic sentiment. Additionally, the integralists fail to recognize that the protections the U.S. Constitution offers to religious groups that do not share their faith are the same ones that protect Catholics from the tyranny of these groups. Were these safeguards not in place, intolerant American Protestants would have sent millions of Irish, German, Polish, and Italian Catholic immigrants back to their home countries in the nineteenth and early twentieth centuries. My Catholic university might never have been founded!

Finally, so-called postliberal Catholics propose that the Church can find her deserved place in American society if citizens can be persuaded to abandon liberal democracy and entrust their future to an enlightened aristocracy. This solution would be great, if only we could guarantee the rule of virtuous leaders who are committed to the common good. However, as hapless citizens have repeatedly found in the centuries after the French Revolution, there is often a big and bloody difference between the utopian promises of a countercultural elite and how it acts when it gains total power.

Though I regard these arguments with bemused skepticism, all three would probably seem downright strange to the rising generation of young Catholics, the so-called Gen Z (born between 1997 and 2012), on whose support the Church's credibility in the future will depend. If orthodox Catholic intellectuals think the "Zoomers" in my classroom will be inspired by these ideas to devote their energy to raising the Church's profile, they will be disappointed. After all, these students belong to a social cohort in which all forms of institutional authority are under fire. Because far more people are flying out of established churches than entering them, Gen Z has become the least religious generation ever. More than one-third of those who were raised as churchgoers now say that they have no religious affiliation at all. A majority of all Zoomers see no particular benefit in raising children in any religious tradition.[1] Overall, they reflect a trend that has been underway among all Catholic generations, especially those born since the 1970s. Since 2007 alone, the share of the U.S. population that self-identifies as Catholic has fallen from twenty-four percent to nineteen percent in 2023–2024. Correspondingly, the percentage of all Americans who now describe their religious affiliation as "nothing in particular" is the same (nineteen percent).[2] This is a striking development given the fact that the U.S. has long been significantly more religious than other advanced democracies.

Most of my Zoomer students have not taken part in this exodus. Yet, they are no more inclined than their non-believing peers to be attracted to facile experiments with alternate realities. The majority do not regard the American experiment with liberal democracy as a failure, let alone a threat to their faith. They regard it as a success story and are aghast when self-serving politicians show disdain for the rule of law. Accordingly, they expect Church leaders to come to the defense of this system and its underlying values. Some of them are Democrats, roughly equal numbers are Republicans. Regardless of these partisan differences, they all want the representatives of their faith to be voices of reason and moderation in an unnecessarily polarized society. They want the Church to call out politicians' lies about supposedly rigged elections and a nonexistent Deep State. Because they value expertise and accept the scientific method, they expect her leaders to denounce all forms of

[1] Daniel A. Cox, "Generation Z and the Future of Faith in America," American Survey Center (March 24, 2022), https://www.americansurveycenter.org/research/generation-z-future-of-faith.

[2] Gregory Smith, et al., Pew Research Center, "Religious Identity" (Feb. 26, 2025), https://www.pewresearch.org/religion/2025/02/26/religious-landscape-study-religious-identity.

pseudo-scientific quackery and denialism. For example, like roughly six out of ten members of their generation, they regard global climate change as one of the greatest existential threats to humanity and are determined to see its causes addressed.[3] Most importantly, my students expect the Church to be a tireless advocate of Christ's command to honor the dignity of every human being, regardless of trivial differences in race, ethnicity, or nationality.

Do these attitudes confirm, as some orthodox Catholic intellectuals bemoan, that the Zoomers have fallen under the sway of a pernicious liberal establishment? Worse still, has a radical leftist professoriate brainwashed them into abandoning their faith? This does not appear to be the case with Catholic students at the University of Notre Dame. Quite the contrary, my students welcome the opportunity to discuss their faith in the classroom. I am happy to oblige! They regularly attend the more than one hundred and sixty Masses that are celebrated on our campus every week. Their dorm chapels are jampacked. They enthusiastically take part in the hundreds of service activities sponsored by our Institute for Social Concerns. Many go on to earn teaching degrees from our Alliance for Catholic Education, which has sent thousands of our graduates into America's poorest Catholic schools.

In many ways, what I experience on a regular basis is good news for anyone who worries about the marginalization of Catholicism in America. Admittedly, my students are not typical representatives of their generation in every respect. The process of self-selection that goes into choosing to attend Notre Dame makes them more likely to have a positive disposition toward their faith than their peers at other elite universities. Yet, this difference is a positive indication that they and other young Catholics will be up to the

---

[3] Emily Sullivan, "Millennials and Gen Z Sound the Alarm on Climate Change," *Global Affairs* (Jan. 18, 2023), https://globalaffairs.org/commentary-and-analysis/blogs/millennials-and-gen-z-sound-alarm-climate-change.

challenge of breathing new life into the Church. If anything, it is remarkable that they have not already given up on their faith. Let us remember that these Zoomers have grown up in an era haunted by the sexual abuse scandals of the clergy. Thus, it is understandable that many have ambivalent feelings about the institutional Church. They are not alone; nearly one-quarter of American Catholics say that they attend Mass less often and have reduced their donations because of the scandals.[4] In this light, it is a hopeful sign that these young people have had the strength of character to espouse beliefs that are significantly more meaningful than the self-interested motivations of their peers.

To maintain Gen Z's enthusiasm for the Church, orthodox Catholics must recognize that they cannot afford to marginalize themselves by holing up in self-satisfied ideological bubbles. Rather than complaining about the Zoomers' alleged shortcomings or lecturing them about how they should vote, we must dedicate ourselves to presenting the Church as an institution that is worthy of these young people's trust. After all, Gen Z has come of age in a world we created. We can't blame the Church's current trials on the Zoomers. If orthodox Catholics recognize that it is up to them to act on this opportunity, they will stand a good chance of winning the hearts and souls of a generation that is in the position to renew the Church's credibility as a force for good in American life.

∞ ∞ ∞

A. James McAdams *is the William M. Scholl Professor of International Affairs at the University of Notre Dame and a contributing editor of the* New Oxford Review. *He is the author of numerous books, including* Vanguard of the Revolution: The Global Idea of the Communist Party *(Princeton University Press).*

---

[4] "Americans See Catholic Clergy Sex Abuse as an Ongoing Problem," Pew Research Center (June 11, 2019), https://www.pewresearch.org/religion/2019/06/11/americans-see-catholic-clergy-sex-abuse-as-an-ongoing-problem.

7

A Laughable Proposition

PRESTON R. SIMPSON

THERE ARE SEVERAL PROBLEMS with the set of questions in this symposium. Most Americans would laugh at the question of whether there is any hope for Catholics in American political life. The outgoing president is a Catholic, the leader of the Democratic Party in the House of Representatives for twenty years until 2023 was a Catholic, and a majority of the U.S. Supreme Court justices are Catholics. The question of whether Catholics can expect a "place at the table" of American politics is nonsensical unless it means something other than what an ordinary American would consider a Catholic. Who are these Catholics who seek a "place at the table," where much of the power is already held by people who identify as Catholics?

As I am not a Catholic, I can only make an educated guess. I assume the question defines Catholics as those who adhere to the traditional teachings of the Catholic Church — who reject, for example, abortion, *in vitro* fertilization, artificial contraception, transsexualism, and remarriage after divorce, and who would like to see these prohibitions enforced in civil society. Furthermore, they believe the Roman pontiff is infallible when speaking on faith and morals and, therefore, could command the obedience of ruling American Catholics to unknown future moral pronouncements. Would these hypothetical pronouncements have the force of law in American life? As people who self-define as Catholics have widely divergent views on moral issues, this prospect is anathema to the vast majority of Americans, including, undoubtedly, many (most?) who call themselves Catholic. Indeed, John F. Kennedy, when he ran for president in 1960, had to assure his countrymen that he was not beholden to the Church.

The question of whether the American experiment is an exhausted project is difficult to answer. Certainly, some developments suggest it is. When the presidential candidate of one of the two major parties makes it her signature issue that women should be allowed to kill their children; when mainstream medicine endorses chemical and surgical mutilation of children who are temporarily confused about their sexual identity; when many leaders and would-be leaders desire a completely open and unregulated border; and when many politicians and academics claim that freedom of speech is a dangerous and outmoded idea (to name only a few disturbing developments of recent years), there certainly is concern for the future of the enterprise.

America has been through and survived severe divisions in the past. The American Revolution was, in some respects, a civil war. In the period around the War of 1812, there was not insignificant talk of secession by Northeastern states. From 1861 to 1865 there was an actual attempt at secession by Southern states, eventuating in a very bloody Civil War. Yet America survived those events and emerged as the leading power in the world and a beacon of freedom to people across the globe.

The biggest problem with the symposium questions is that they rest on a false assumption. They seem to assume that "the American experiment" has some relation to the Catholic Church. But the American experiment was never a Catholic project. You could almost say it was an anti-Catholic project. Nearly all the founders were Protestants, Deists, or Unitarians. Only one Catholic signed the Declaration of Independence, and only three signed the Constitution. The Roman Church is a monarchical organization headed by someone with nearly absolute power over the organization. The American experiment is a complete rejection of that principle. It assumes that ordinary citizens (think of them as the people in the pews) have the ability and should have the power to choose their leaders, participate in the making of laws, and serve on juries. And yet, over its history, millions of Catholics from Italy, Ireland, Poland, and countless other places have fled their Catholic homelands to participate in the non-Catholic American system.

If the Catholics addressed in the questions desire a truly Catholic society, it will not be the United States of America as presently constituted. And if the American experiment is to survive and flourish, it will need to find people of integrity, vision, and persuasiveness like Washington, Madison, Lincoln, and Reagan — none of whom was Catholic or even particularly religious. Catholics need to decide if they are willing to work within the present system, which may well degenerate into totalitarianism. But the Catholics here in the United States have, along with those of other faiths and no faith, already rejected rule by the Roman Catholic Church.

∝ ∝ ∝

PRESTON R. SIMPSON, M.D., *is a retired pathologist who lives in Plano, Texas.*

8

Moral Credibility and the Temptation to Power

MARK BARRETT

N 1928, THE NATION'S FIRST CATH-
olic presidential candidate, Governor Al Smith of
New York, nicknamed "the happy warrior" for
his relentless optimism, was greeted by burning crosses as
his campaign train crossed America. The Ku Klux Klan
organized against him, spreading a rumor that a photo-
graph of him opening the Holland Tunnel in New York
was a tunnel to Rome to facilitate the arrival of the pope.
Another rumor claimed that all Protestant marriages would
be annulled under a Smith administration. Still another
claimed that Smith would open the nation's borders to
hordes of Eastern and Southern Europeans immigrants.
The Birth Control Review warned of "tyrannical intolerance
and usurpation of power exercised by officeholders born
and bred in the Roman Catholic faith." Smith's opponent,
Herbert Hoover, hypocritically paid lip-service to opposing
all prejudice, while his campaign co-operated with it. Signs
asking, "For Hoover and America, or for Smith and Rome.
Which?" dotted the countryside. Hoover's campaign was
not troubled by this framing. Nor were many elite institutions. Charles C. Marshall, an Episcopalian lawyer, asked
in an open letter in *The Atlantic Monthly* whether there
was an "irrepressible conflict" between Smith's Catholic
faith and the U.S. Constitution. More eloquent than the
signs, but the basic idea is the same.

Before launching his campaign, Smith rejected the idea
that he would be subject to religious prejudice. But he
eventually admitted that his faith was a political problem

and confronted the issue. First, he responded to Marshall's letter in the same venue, highlighting the disingenuous nature of many of the charges and patiently refuting the logic of others. Second, in a campaign speech in Oklahoma City, the heart of Klan country, he condemned as sacrilege the burning of the cross of Christ as a symbol of hate, and he described the attacks on his religion as pure bigotry and intolerance. In neither forum did he back away from his faith.

Smith lost, decisively. A Democrat, he lost counties that had never voted Republican before and would not again for many decades. Though many factors worked against Smith — importantly, he forcefully opposed prohibition — the shape and scale of the defeat point to his faith as the biggest problem. The prejudice he had experienced shocked and traumatized Smith. The campaign soured him on the American experiment, at least for a time. He grew bitter and questioned the country's commitment to its own constitutional principles. By one account, his opposition to many of the programs he had once championed as governor, when presented as national policy in the New Deal, stemmed in part from his sense that a nation so corrupted by prejudice could not be trusted with such power.

Smith loved his country, but it had scorned him, and he responded as scorned lovers often do. He had good reason to feel betrayed by America's failure to live up to its promises, but he should not have been surprised. Nor should we. The argument that Catholics do not fully belong in America, whether in its sophisticated or vulgar form, presents itself differently now than in 1928, but it still lurks in the background of our political discussions. Recognition of this reality is no bad thing if it enhances the integrity of our witness and our moral credibility. But it is easy to lose our perspective. We may be tempted to wed our faith to political agendas that seem to offer protection and power. The media-industrial complex cultivates and profits from such temptations, trading on anger and fear.

Politicians seeking to benefit from this phenomenon are legion. The battle against faith's becoming the servant of power is one that must be renewed constantly.

Yet, as Smith despaired, other Catholics, inspired by his impressive record, were addressing the needs of their communities. While they lamented their exclusion from elite institutions, they did not see this as an impediment to promoting the well-being of their neighbors. These efforts most often began in the local community, whether in urban neighborhoods or in factories and mines through the burgeoning labor movement. Primarily focused on the material needs of individuals and families, their efforts helped to obtain jobs, feed widows and children, welcome and integrate immigrants into society, abolish child labor, secure collective-bargaining rights, and establish the outlines of a social-insurance system. Far from signaling a retreat from the world, this presaged the New Deal order to come, the contours of which Catholics would help to shape.

Neoliberalism and a "throwaway culture" present a new set of problems to solve, and the commodification of everything, from human life to labor, demands a response from Catholics — a response that, if faithful, will confound both the Left and the Right. The issues today are different, but not that different. The disparity between the wealthiest and the rest of the population today has returned to levels not seen since the early twentieth century. The working class and middle class still face struggles related to job insecurity, stagnant wages, and a rising cost of living. The "gig economy" and the erosion of traditional labor rights present questions as to how workers can most effectively exercise their right to organize and secure a living wage. The wealthiest and most politically powerful section of society, now the Silicon Valley techno-libertarian elite, once again unabashedly promotes eugenics.

As Smith and other Catholics knew a century ago, our political choices shape the economy, which, in turn, shapes society. What should be equally clear to us today is that the choices made over the past several decades have enriched a few and exacerbated a range of social issues that may appear unrelated, such as delayed or failed marriages, the rise of non-marriage, the decline of civic organizations, and the increase in identity politics and political polarization.

When first confronted with Marshall's article, Smith is alleged to have remarked, "What the hell is an encyclical?" Whether or not he and our forebears read the papal encyclicals, they applied a distinctly Catholic conception of the world to the questions of the day. They did not throw up their hands in the face of bigotry and exclusion. Nor did they retreat. Rather, they went about the hard work of figuring out how to love their neighbors and seek the common good in the realm of public law and policy. Their work testifies to their convictions. We are the inheritors of their precious legacy, if we remember it.

∞ ∞ ∞

MARK BARRETT *is a Pittsburgh lawyer and historian of the Ancient Order of Hibernians, Division 32, in Carnegie, Pennsylvania.*

9

No Faith, No Future

CHARLES A. COULOMBE

AVING LIVED FOR THE PAST SEVEN years in Austria, I am in an interesting position of having gained a deeper understanding of our mother continent and the various countries from which the majority of the inhabitants of the United States come *and* a correspondingly deeper love for the land of my birth. Rather than a "shining city on a hill" or the "last best hope of mankind," she is the country in which I was born, by God's will. She has been very kind to my family and me, and I have a sacred duty toward her—patriotism being a religious virtue. As I am a Catholic, and she a non-Catholic country, part of that duty is to try to evangelize her. She did not begin in 1776 with the Declaration of Independence, or even in 1492, but in 1567 with the establishment of permanent European settlements on her soil. This is to say, her history is not merely that of her independent political institutions but of her colonial roots in Spain, France, and Britain. If those institutions should change radically, she would still be the country I love.

With that in mind, I cannot say whether the "American experiment" failed or succeeded because I do not believe in the concept. I believe in these United States. That they have declined culturally, morally, religiously, and politically in my lifetime is undeniable, as is the fact that the era of Irving Berlin and Norman Rockwell in which I first saw the light is gone beyond recall. But the country remains; even if she were to be dismembered like Austria-Hungary, a great deal would remain of her in the successor states to which her end would give rise. Were her Catholics energetic enough to convert her, she would become a great nation indeed, whatever shape her virtue would impress upon her institutions. Unless and until then, she shall flounder as she always has — and yet I shall love her until I die.

The necessity of conversion is not only individual, for each soul, but for the well-being of the country as a whole. Orestes Brownson knew this when he wrote, "The Roman Catholic religion, then, is necessary to sustain popular liberty, because popular liberty can be sustained only by a religion free from popular control, above the people, speaking from above and able to command them, — and such a religion is the Roman Catholic."[1] Without the faith, the First Republic, as we might call the period of American history from 1783 to 1860, collapsed. So fell what we might call the Second Republic (1865–1941). From the Second World War emerged the First Empire, which is with us yet. But because we have failed to evangelize the nation, we Catholics have never had a place at the table, for the most part; nor have we deserved it, really.

Nevertheless, the accidents of history have made Catholics a majority in certain areas of the country: southern Louisiana, northern New Mexico, and various ethnic islands scattered throughout the Midwest, Northeast, and elsewhere. If the U.S. bishops ever regain a strong grip on the faith, they would be in a position to exert a strong influence in certain localities. During the "Black Mass at Harvard" episode in 2014, I was one of a thousand who marched in a Eucharistic procession from the chapel at Massachusetts Institute of Technology to St. Paul's Church in Harvard Square, protesting the proposed satanic rite. There we joined a like number who were engaged in a holy hour of reparation. All this was arranged by the extremely able Catholic chaplaincy at Harvard University. It occurred to me as we marched, and cars honked in support and people dropped to their knees in the street, that the faith

---

[1] "Catholicity Necessary to Sustain Popular Liberty," *Brownson's Quarterly Review* (Oct. 1845).

is far from dead in the Boston area—it just lacks real leadership. Had the archbishop of Boston stood up for the faith regularly as the Harvard chaplains did that day, politics in the Bay State would be considerably different. But so long as we are burdened by those who hid under their beds and abandoned their flocks during COVID, we shall have the conditions we have.

The question of what we should do in the face of the current situation is really the same one with which our ancestors grappled, and which they spectacularly failed to answer. Neither the formation of "intentional communities" nor political tinkering is going to solve the American conundrum; it is, in any case, a false argument because strategies should be seen as differing means toward the same end, rather than either-or propositions. So, too, the debate over integralism, wherein some see it as the threat of imposing "Catholic sharia" on an unwilling populace—which it most certainly would be today, given the infanticidal propensities of a majority of Americans. But abortion was not outlawed in ancient Rome until after its conversion—nor shall it be here. The medieval and early modern order to which the integralists look for inspiration was not purpose-built. Rather, as the peoples of Europe and elsewhere converted, their institutions organically altered in accordance with their populations' new religion, and so was born Christendom. So, too, shall it be with the wonderful country God has given us, if ever American Catholics—clerical and lay—do their patriotic and religious duty and work toward her conversion (while not neglecting any necessary political efforts). That is the great hope for Catholic Americans, and for our country.

∞ ∞ ∞

CHARLES A. COULOMBE *is a contributing editor of* CrisisMagazine.com *(and its European correspondent),* OnePeterFive.com, *and* The European Conservative. *He previously served as a columnist for the* Catholic Herald *and film critic for the* National Catholic Register. *A celebrated historian, his books include* Puritan's Empire: A Catholic Perspective on American History, Star-Spangled Crown: A Simple Guide to the American Monarchy, Blessed Charles of Austria: A Holy Emperor and His Legacy, *and most recently,* Zita: Empress of Austria and Queen of Hungary. *He resides in Vienna, Austria, and Los Angeles, California.*

10

"The Future's so Bright…"

CHRISTOPHER BEITING

MY FATHER WAS A BOY DURING World War II, and when I was a boy myself, I once asked him what that experience had been like.

"Scary" he said.

"Why?" I asked.

"Hey, we didn't know we were going to win!" he replied.

As we Catholics look forward to an increasingly difficult time in American public and political life, I think it is important to keep my father's words in mind.

How do we know we're *not* going to win?

The late Francis Cardinal George, former archbishop of Chicago, once famously said, "I expect to die in bed, my successor will die in prison, and his successor will die a martyr in the public square." A friend of mine once met Cardinal George and asked him directly, "Did you really mean that?"

"Yes, I did," the Cardinal replied, "But everybody always forgets the last part of what I said: 'But his successor will pick up the shards of a ruined society and slowly help rebuild civilization, as the Church has done so often in human history.'"

When we live through difficult times, it is easy to forget better ones and overlook the fact that we have empirical evidence for some things. As proof of the point the cardinal was trying to make, consider the history of the Church in France. After the persecutions during the French Revolution and the Napoleonic era, the Church was in dire shape, with closed churches, devastated religious orders, and few clergy. In a country of some thirty million people, there were only around twelve thousand nuns and three thousand priests left. Any honest observer of the situation would not have seemed unreasonable for predicting the extinction of Catholicism in France. However, that con-clusion did not factor in the work of the Holy Spirit—or the remarkable regenerative power of an institution whose Founder Himself rose from the dead. By 1878 there were about one hundred and thirty-five thousand nuns and thirty thousand priests in France—more than a tenfold increase in a matter of a few decades.

Pondering facts like these, and the words of the good car-dinal, has led my friend to quip frequently, "We Catholics are like cockroaches; there's no getting rid of us for long."

In lieu of a consideration of the future of Catholics in American public life, I would like to consider some-thing more fundamental, and speculate about the future of Catholicism in America, since there will be no role for Catholics in American public life if there is no func-tioning Catholic Church in America. To do this, I would like to focus not on the current situation of Catholicism in America (where things are a mess), or that of the near future (where things look like they may get worse), but that period about which Cardinal George spoke: the time of great rebuilding, the light after the darkness. Of course, no one truly knows the future but the Father in Heaven, and it is difficult to say whether the events of the 2024 election will represent a true and lasting sea change for the United States as a whole or just a temporary reprieve for, or miti-gation of, an inevitable time of persecution for Catholics in particular. Nevertheless, a number of things—very positive things—are already happening in the Church in America which are not always obvious and which, if they continue, hold the promise of many good things in the future.

The first trend has to do with changes in church mem-bership, which is happening not just in Catholicism but in many Christian denominations in this country, and which is paradoxical in nature.

Sociologists have commented on the latest trend in the never-ending "battle of the sexes," which is that American women are becoming increasingly "liberal," and American men increasingly "conservative." This trend has numerous ramifications, but I would like to focus on what it means for church membership. Sociologists have contended that while church membership in America is in decline overall, the decline is steepest among young women, who appear to be leaving churches in droves. Yet, while this is happening, there is a parallel trend of young men increasingly *joining* churches. It is not hard to grasp why this is happening. If the ideology of modernity in general, and feminism in particular, disparages men and masculinity (which it does and has been doing for a long time), many men will not only *not* be attracted to it but will reject it and seek alternatives. Moreover, given the social and personal anomie in which many young men find themselves these days, it is not surprising that they are following the advice of the Jordan Petersons of the world and looking for ways to pull their lives together. Joining a church, particularly a "conservative" one, is a good way to do that.

My personal experience bears this out. A few years ago, I did a favor for a nun who ran the religion department of a local Catholic high school and filled in for a year for another teacher. Many of the classes I taught were for seniors, and most of the students were male. I found that having attended an all-male Catholic high school myself back in the day served me in good stead in dealing with my often-fractious charges. But I was continually surprised by how many of the senior guys I taught were socially and politically conservative, and consciously Catholic as well — much more so than the guys at my own high school were, way back when.

Assuming this male/female trend in church membership continues, it has a lot of implications for the future of Catholicism in America. Any sociologist of religion can tell you that, for a long time now, though Christian churches have been run by males, the majority of the active parishioners, particularly in church matters and ministries, have been females. If women are doing something, chances are men won't do it, which is as true for church ministries as it is for sports, education, and even housework (ask my wife). As a result, Christian churches in America often have a "feminized" character, whether wittingly or unwittingly, and Catholic churches are no exception to this trend.

What will happen to the practices and character of churches when the gender dynamic shifts and the congregations become predominantly male? How appealing will schmaltzy, sentimentalized hymns and etiolated, femmy blonde images of Jesus be to an increasingly masculine congregation? Not very, I would argue. Instead, I suspect we will see a shift to a more "muscular Christianity" approach to the faith that will appeal more to men — and have the added benefit of being better suited to a Church undergoing overt persecution.

Moreover, there is a hidden benefit to this masculinization process that could prove very significant. Many of the restless young men who are joining Christian churches in order to get their lives together will naturally want to start families as part of this process, and when these earnest lads start looking for godly marriage prospects in their newfound parishes, they may be in for a bit of a disappointment. If they are serious about marriage, they are likely going to have to settle for unchurched women, and if they are serious about their faith, they are going to drag their unchurched wives to church with them in the hope of converting them. But here again, any sociologist of religion is going to tell you that the *single most important determining factor* in ensuring that children go on to practice their faith as adults is having a father who practices his faith. Many Catholic men's groups these days are *implicitly* based on this assumption. These trends augur well for a future role of prominence for Catholicism in American public life.

Moreover, with regard to Catholicism, this masculinizing trend is already underway, as I can again confirm from first-hand experience. There are now a wide variety of Catholic men's programs available at most parishes across the country (a number of which I have participated in personally), with any number of new ones in the works. I can also offer anecdotal evidence from a statewide Catholic conference my wife and I attended last year. I was expecting an attendance of about four hundred, and I was stunned to find it was more than ten times that, with many, if not most, of the attendees being men. I was also surprised by the merch on sale by the vendors — I frankly lost count of the number of T-shirts and hoodies featuring St. Benedict medallions, St. Michael the Archangel, St. Joseph, and other aggressively masculine images and themes. Nor have I myself proven immune to this trend. I've spent the past fifty-plus years of praying with a rosary my mother gave me for my First Communion, and I never expected that to change. But last Lent I picked up an extra rosary for "concealed carry" purposes (it's a Knights of Columbus thing), and the one I got was made of gunmetal and patterned after rosaries carried by soldiers in World War I. I have been surprised by how much I use my new one in place of my treasured old one. The new one feels somehow . . . better . . . in my hands. Sorry, Mom.

The second trend I wish to mention has to do with the nature of the young priests fresh out of seminary.

It has been my pleasure to work directly with about six of these guys over the past few years, and I have been very impressed by them — and grown more in my spiritual life under their ministry than at any other time in my life. I thought I was just lucky, or specially blessed by God, but when articles came out in the Catholic press not long ago surveying the population in America's seminaries and concluding that there simply *aren't* any progressives or liberals in Catholic seminaries, I realized that what I thought was an exception was, in fact, the rule. Here again, the situation makes sense: socially, there is simply no upside — and plenty of downsides — to being a Catholic priest these days, so the only guys who are drawn to the priesthood are the ones who are there for The Right Reasons. Lord knows, there are nowhere near enough of them, and we laity in the pews are in for some lean years, priest-wise, in the near future. But what we are losing in quantity we are more than making up for in quality.

There's more. The articles about the composition of today's seminaries note that if seminarians admit to a problem, it is a lack of trust in their bishops, which leaves most of the people with whom I've shared these articles feeling pretty bad about the state of Church. But they shouldn't. I explained it to my wife, who was depressed by the news, as follows: "Nah, nah, forget the bishops thing, dear — you're missing the Big Picture. Think. If the *only* thing coming out of seminaries these days are guys the likes of our pastor, Fr. Andrew, what is the Church in America going to be like when *every* priest is a Fr. Andrew?"

"Oh," she replied.

"Remember: the old guard isn't going to last forever. What is the Church in America going to be like when that crowd is gone, and every *bishop* is a Fr. Andrew as well?"

"Ohhhh…," she replied.

Yeah. *Ohhhh*, indeed.

Moreover, it's also worth wondering what is going to happen when these particular trends — and others — start becoming synergistic and building on each other.

Good things, I expect.

Sure, things are dark for the Church in America right now, and they may likely get darker — only the Father can say for sure. But it is abundantly clear to me that the Church is already starting to get the congregations — and the leadership — she is going to need to see her through any dark times ahead and begin the process of rebuilding about which Cardinal George spoke. It happened in France in the nineteenth century, as it has so many times before, and it can happen here.

And when it does, those days are going to be *very* bright indeed.

Right now, I feel like Simeon holding an infant Messiah he would never see grow to manhood, or Moses gazing at a Promised Land he would never be able to enter. I will not live long enough to see those bright days for the Church in America. But some of you younger people who are reading this will.

And I envy you.

∞ ∞ ∞

CHRISTOPHER BEITING *is archivist at Waldorf University, editor-in-chief of* The Catholic Social Science Review, *and a contributing editor of the* New Oxford Review.

11

Decision and Indecision, Hope and Hopelessness

KARL KEATING

O N CHRISTMAS DAY 1886, EIGHTEEN-year-old Paul Claudel—brought up Catholic but delinquent in his faith—was listening to Vespers in Notre-Dame de Paris. "I stood near the second pillar at the entrance to the chancel, to the right, on the side of the sacristy," he later recounted. "Then occurred the event which dominates my entire life. In an instant my heart was touched, and I believed. I believed with such a strength of adherence, with such an uplifting of my entire being, with such powerful conviction, with such a certainty leaving no room for any kind of doubt, that since then all the books, all the arguments, all the incidents and accidents of a busy life have been unable to shake my faith." Claudel would go on to a long diplomatic career, becoming the French consul in many countries and eventually ambassador to Japan and, from 1928 to 1933, to the United States. He achieved fame as a poet and playwright, but he was not yet famous when, in 1907, he received a letter from twenty-year-old Jacques Rivière.

The young man was in a sorrier state, religiously, than Claudel had been before his 1886 reversion. Rivière was full of passion and doubt. "I seem to see Christianity dying," he wrote. "Indeed, none of us know what has happened to it. Nor what to make of those spires above the roofs of our great towns which symbolize no longer the prayer of any of us. Nor the meaning today of those great fabrics, hemmed in by railway stations and hospitals, and from which the people themselves have driven the monks. Nor what those stucco crosses, disfigured by an abominable art, that stand above the graves in our cemeteries, would tell us."

Rivière felt himself lost and ardently wished to be found. He and Claudel exchanged letters for years, Rivière asymptotically coming closer to peace within the Church and then veering off, repeatedly, into despair. He became a noted writer, editor, and critic. He never settled comfortably in the faith — his was a perpetually incomplete conversion, it seemed — and he died of typhoid in 1925. Writing two years after Rivière's death, his widow said that "he was honest as some men are dark-haired or snub-nosed" and that "he believed that when others spoke of their sins, they, like himself, were referring to their temptations."

Well before he wrote his first, plaintive letter to his hero Claudel, Rivière was infected by that French philosophical malaise that produced so many fine but dead-end writers in the late-nineteenth and early twentieth centuries. He never acted sufficiently on Claudel's superb advice to him: "Read Dante. And as much as you can find of Newman." And Chesterton, whom Claudel greatly admired.

I mention Claudel and Rivière at length because for me they symbolize the hope and (seeming) hopelessness of our current situation. Claudel shows the possibility of a quick and lasting change, Rivière the possibility of prolonged indecision and inertia.

Sometimes I say, in private or in public, "I'm an optimist. I'm *positive* that things will get worse." The quip elicits a chuckle — or at least a smirk. People know what I mean. Both sides of the comment are true. I do think things will get worse, in certain ways and in the short term, but I also think "this too shall pass." While I do not expect to live long enough see Churchillian sunlit uplands, I may live long enough to be able to say, with a knowing smile, "I told you so."

At times I share the frustration and pessimism of Rivière, at other times the calm and assurance of Claudel. Mostly, I am with the latter. I do think some things will get worse — some perhaps uncomfortably worse — but I have enough confidence in providential superintendence that I expect the worsening to be countervailed by a bettering. I am old enough to have seen sufficient examples. Though I never lived near it — I have lived in Southern California rather than in the South — I remember racial segregation. I remember when it was disappearing, with glacial slowness. One had the sense that its final demise would occur but only in the distant future. And then, in a generation, it was gone, along with all sympathy for it. It wasn't so much that laws had changed but that hearts and minds had changed, more quickly than most people expected. I have seen parallel things in matters of religion.

I worked in Catholic apologetics for more than four decades and still dabble in it. I engaged lifelong anti-Catholics in public debates, and I dealt one-on-one in private with countless diehard opponents of the Church, both religious and secular. I dealt with Catholics more lukewarm than Jacques Rivière or more misinformed than internet pundits. I learned much through these interactions, and one thing I learned is not to despair. I have seen too many conversions — religious, civic, cultural — for that. Some have been gradual, others instantaneous. Many have been inexplicable, yet they occurred. I learned not to put trust in princes, whether ecclesiastical or political, because they almost invariably disappoint. I am skeptical of schemes, no matter how well reasoned or intentioned. I particularly am averse to sentimentalistic or romantic schemes, because of their impracticality. For that reason I give little attention to, for example, the Catholic integralist movement. While its logic may seem to stick together ("Who says A must say B," said Lenin), there is no real chance of its coming into play, at least not in this century. You cannot have a Catholic integralist society unless the society already is overwhelmingly Catholic — and convictedly so. In our wildest hopes, we are nowhere near that. The solution to current woes will need to be found elsewhere.

But now I have misspoken, because there is no solution, at least not here below. There is only amelioration. Perhaps I have undiscovered British genes: I think we can muddle along, deleting much, repairing much, not despairing, but not fantasizing.

∞ ∞ ∞

KARL KEATING *has engaged in Catholic apologetics for more than four decades. He is a contributing editor of the* New Oxford Review *and the author of twenty books. His most recent is* 1054 and All That: A Lighthearted History of the Catholic Church.

12

Orthodoxy and Beauty—
Forget the Rest

GRACJAN KRASZEWSKI

HE AMERICAN EXPERIMENT IS NOT an exhausted project. Despite a vicious Civil War that temporarily birthed a second American nation, albeit a short-lived one, a roughhewn closure of the frontier as announced by Frederick Jackson Turner in Chicago in 1893, with Native American displacements and wars and the tragic legacy of slavery not that far in the past, and an "American Century" that would include two devastating global conflicts (the first one the most significant geopolitical event of the past five hundred years) and melioristic adventurism(s) in Latin America, Southeast Asia, and the Middle East before drawing to a close—the twentieth century, that is, the Fukuyama/*Friends*/Coca-Cola End of History 1990s, more specifically—on September 10, 2001, the American experiment is not an exhausted project.

Poland was thrice partitioned and then wiped off the map only to reappear with redrawn and malleable borders. Russia experienced an apocalypse in 1917 and has yet to recover. France died in 1789. The sun long ago set on the British Empire. America has yet to reach two hundred and fifty years, so perhaps such comparisons are myopic, if not plainly unfair. But the point remains. America, for whatever reason—luck? gumption? the can-do spirit? Midwest manners as can be found in central Illinois? God having truly shed His grace on thee, on us?—has traversed this ongoing time from its founding until now exceptionally peaceful and intact. Exceptionally peaceful even though we have been, technically, at war more often than at peace.

Intact is more relevant anyways. America has had many an opportunity to be carved up by secession, internal revolution, avaricious westward expansion, domestic disturbances, and economic depletions from foreign wars. But it has not been. We should not gloss over the fact, nor forget to marvel at the fact, that a map of contiguous forty-eight American states looks exactly the same in June 2025, as it did on August 26, 1987, and April 14, 1962, and March 16, 1922, and Valentine's Day 1912 (the day Arizona became the forty-eighth state to join the Union, two years before the Great War, two months before the *Titanic* sank).

One hundred and thirteen years of ongoing territorial integrity measured down to the last square inch, itself built on one hundred and thirty-seven years of progress in this direction minus fracturing cataclysms, is no small matter. But far more important is the American idealistic-ideological tradition that has endured for two hundred and fifty years. Yes, Eugene Debs; and the tumultuous 1960s; and Cold War ducking under desks, fearing the end of it all wrapped around that. This essay began with the American Civil War, after all. But no one can seriously argue that Debs and American socialists, even during the Great Depression, posed a Bolshevik-like threat. No one thinks America came close to some kind of dissolution around the time of Watergate, Woodstock, and four dead in Ohio. America — once more, why? It is hard to say why — has endured, both territorially and idealistically. "Freedom" and "Liberty" and "Fairness" and "Hard Work" and "Give Me Your Huddled Masses" and the "Land of Opportunity" and "Democracy" — especially "Making the World Safe for Democracy" — are, without question, often cloying, fake, and wholly empty slogans. When someone wears them on a T-shirt the nauseating effect is increased. And yet people do, and have, for two hundred and fifty years, believed these things in one form or another. They are born here and so born into, or come here, for these very same clichés, which, to them, to us, are lights to live by. The American experiment is not an exhausted project.

Yes, there is hope for Catholics in American political life. It has always been here. That Catholics have been historically marginalized, or are at present marginalized, is greatly exaggerated. Yes, the Know Nothings and the KKK hated Catholics. They also hated plenty of other groups besides. There will always be some guy in some backwoods holler somewhere yelling calumnies about the pope, papists, and Romanism. Considering it is not certain this same man can count to ten or even read the Bible he claims to follow faithfully, maybe less attention should be paid here? Burning convents in the antebellum North is bad—I hope that goes without saying—but for every anti-Catholic arsonist there were scores more of pro-Catholic Protestants, especially in the American South, helping build, fund, and support Catholic schools and hospitals. America has never had a Jewish, Muslim, Buddhist, or Mormon president. We have had two Catholic ones, and should the next fifty years, let's say, produce a long run of *only* Catholic presidents, I do not think many people would be surprised.

America has always been a "WASP" country. If anything is today marginalized, threatened, or in decline, it is the grand institutional Protestant churches that had for so long made up the religious backbone of the nation. As everyone knows, Catholics have been the largest single Christian group in America for decades now. The second largest? Former Catholics. I'm saying just the sheer numbers are, and have been, there. To Protestants once more, I want to make clear that though I am not a mathematician or a statistician, I'd venture a guess that it is today a hundred to one in favor of the supercool, backwards hat, prosperity gospeling "pastor" with four private jets leading services at the vanilla-latte "church" compared to anything Jonathan Edwards would approve of. The American experiment is not an exhausted project. There is hope for Catholics in American political life.

But before we discuss what Catholics can and should do, let's discuss what they should *not* do. No, to the Benedict Option. No, to integralism. I'll pause briefly to make a few confessions here, for the purpose of disclosure and transparency. I am a practicing Catholic. May God help me become truly devout and holy. I believe it all, Catholicism. I love the Latin Mass. I think everyone should pray the Rosary and Divine Mercy Chaplet and read the Bible every day. I am not conservative or liberal. I'm just a Catholic, and an American, too, and so I say once more: No, to the Benedict Option, and no to integralism.

We do not need Catholicism to become in any way something like the state church of America. I say this precisely because I love the Church. How many years into such a scenario do you start getting not simply the Investiture Controversy of 1122 but, obviously much worse, Henry VIII-type nonsense? It's awesome if God calls you to become a new St. Thomas More, but something wholly different if you create the conditions you hope lead to your becoming a St. Thomas More. You become at this point no better than the Christian fundamentalists trying to immanentize the Eschaton. Do not follow their example. We are not supposed to seek martyrdom, and even the greatest of saints like Francis of Assisi fell prey to this temptation. No integralism. Catholicism being separate from politics is what allows the only thing on Earth that matters—what St. Padre Pio said the world needed more than the sun—to proceed unimpeded. It is the Holy Mass, infinitely more so than what laws govern the nation, that will ultimately lead us poor pilgrims out of this vale of tears safely into our eternal home, the city of God.

I love St. Benedict. I am convinced *ora et labora* is one of the greatest mottos in human history. If this "option" meant being like the monks in sixth-century Norcia, or St. Anthony and the Desert Fathers of the third and fourth, I'd be enthusiastically supportive. Praying without ceasing? Long and arduous fasts? Forty years on a pillar? Rising in the darkest part of the night to sing most beautifully the glories and praise of God? This might, rather, would, certainly save America and do so much more.

I'm afraid, however, that any such "option" as practiced by twenty-first-century Gen X, millennial, and Gen Z Americans would not too long after community establishment drift away from prayer, fasting, and heavenly contemplations into gossipy homeschool cliques, the men arguing whose nineteenth-century-inspired mustache is better waxed and who can continue speaking *while* lighting his pipe, the women shaming repeat offenders of improper veil etiquette, and the development of rival factions that grow further and further entrenched in their own self-righteousness until one can understand, *Oh, so this is how cities so close like Perugia and Assisi fought pitched battles against one another*.

What, then?

What is a Catholic in America, A.D. 2025, to do? Because the American experiment is not an exhausted project, and Catholics should have hope, and should not fall into the kneejerk solutions of integralism or withdrawal.

So, what, then?

Orthodoxy and beauty, and forget the rest.

Orthodoxy first. Be maximally Catholic; pray, fast, give alms, work at your tasks in due season, confident that God will provide the reward. Believe what the Church teaches and live it. Don't be a "cafeteria Catholic." Know that by focusing on the Mass, daily Mass if you can, and daily prayer, and by God's grace remaining in a state of grace, you'll be doing all that has ever mattered: focusing above all on God's Kingdom, the Kingdom to come, the one "not of this world." Focusing on that higher world will reap benefits in this one, too. For as Scripture says, seek first the Kingdom of God and all else will be added unto you. This adding might include a more Catholic society all around. We should want that, hope for that, and pray and work for that. But without falling into coercive integralist fantasies as much as avoiding the kind of wholesale with-drawals from society where there might, eventually, be no one left to witness to a fallen, broken, often depraved world.

Orthodoxy first, beauty next. If we want people to come to Christ and join His Church, and we do, I don't think anyone serious would or could contest the point that we Catholics have to put forth an attractive vision of what, exactly, we're proposing. I'm not speaking about watering down hard truths, accommodating error, or trying to ride the wave of the latest cultural fads. This has been tried, and the results are in, and they are ghastly. The grade reads F, period.

I am speaking about evangelizing by way of beauty. Imagine the hypothetical lukewarm, somewhere between atheism and agnosticism, more accurately termed neopagan "none." Schoolmarmish moral reprimands in the style of "how dare you, how could you?" do not work. Neither does another Catholic personal faith testimony podcast, a new Catholic think tank in NW DC, a new glossy Catholic magazine. These things are often all talk, no action.

What is needed are new works like Dante's *Divine Comedy*. This is beauty in action. We need new Catho-lic Mozarts, DaVincis, and Michaelangelos. These people didn't do a lot of talking, it seems. They created beauty, and people drank it in and realized the ultimate source was God. Because beauty, like goodness and truth, is a transcendental and can simply be presented without fur-ther comment. This is action, active evangelization. We need new Walker Percys and Flannery O'Connors, and fewer Catholic self-help books, which, once more, are a lot of talk, little action, and less beauty. Catholics should be the best in all walks of life and the most beautiful, too. If Catholics actually believe what they profess to believe, they should tap into God's grace and by His grace go out and get after it. Bake the best bread in town. Be the best public speaker. Teach, beautifully. Catholic athletes: play your sport beautifully. The American spirit of "Freedom" and "Liberty" and "Fairness" and "Hard Work" will see this beauty and claim it for itself, uncoerced, and return to greater faithfulness to God and His laws.

The American experiment is not an exhausted project. There is hope for Catholics in American political life. The fullness of the faith, orthodoxy, and a commitment to authentic beauty are the seeds of that hope, for us and for our country.

∞ ∞ ∞

GRACJAN KRASZEWSKI *is the author of six books including the novels* Thermonuclear Mirth *and* Seraphim and the Dust Plague *and the Civil War history* Catholic Confederates. *His most recent work is the forthcoming novel* Mark and Anna, Models: Postmodern Reflections on the Timeless Wisdom of Saint Augustine of Hippo *(Arouca Press, 2025). Holder of a Ph.D. in history, he is director of intellectual formation at Vandal Catholic in Moscow, Idaho.*

13

The Ship Is Sinking—
Man the Lifeboats!

JUDE RUSSO

T IS THE BINDING TEACHING OF the Church, as articulated in *Quanta cura*, the *Syllabus*, and other documents, that a Catholic confessional state is to be preferred to other arrangements. This follows naturally from the Angelic Doctor's discussion of the laws, a foremost purpose of which is to cultivate true religion among the people. This once-uncontroversial position and the tradition that flows from it, championed by the excellent Fr. Edmund Waldstein, O.Cist., has gotten the moniker "integralism" and caused a fair amount of heartburn, both among its whiggish opponents and its more zealous adherents (more on whom anon). On the theory, though, there is no debate. *Roma locuta est.*

Politics, however, occurs in the realm of history and prudence, where the norm is not the philosopher-king but the short-lived regime of the Thirty Tyrants at Athens. The Church recognizes this and has always recognized this. In the context of the revolutionary strains of Judaism that led to the Bar-Kokhba revolt a generation later, the First Letter of Peter is striking: "For love of the Lord, then, bow to every kind of human authority; to the king, who enjoys the chief power, and to the magistrates who hold his commission to punish criminals and encourage honest men." More recently, in the seventeenth century, the Church declined to renew Pope St. Pius V's bull *Regnans in excelsis*, sanctioning the overthrow of the British monarch.

It is in these prudential terms that the more revolutionary integralists may be dismissed. Catholics, although

America's the largest religious identity group, remain a minority in These States. Even granting a successful overthrow of the current government — a very generous hypothetical concession — true minoritarian rule, even by a group in the "right," is a ticklish thing on the best of days. The salutary example of the Thirty again comes to mind. It is true that America's broadly liberal Constitution and disposition preclude the establishment of a confessional regime (even at the state level, thanks to the Fourteenth Amendment), and this is an inherent defect. (To deny this in the teeth of Church teaching, as certain members of an older generation of Catholic conservatives have, is to become as much of a state-worshiper as the communists whom those same eminences see creeping around every corner.) There are also worse things on offer, and those liberal institutions afford certain weapons for advancing just causes. Nor do they seem to be going anywhere any time soon.

Political disengagement doesn't seem to offer much, either. "Intentional communities," à la *The Benedict Option* of my onetime colleague Rod Dreher, are well and good but tend to suffer from two weaknesses: first, an inability to defend themselves in the face of a truly hostile regime, and, second, the material difficulties of establishing a stable community. Founding a successful polity is a hard thing; this is why founders and lawgivers are honored with statues and, in antiquity, divine rites. American history is littered with the ruins of failed communes, and the Leviathan, even in its senescence, is tremendously powerful. Even a glancing blow from it in its death throes can bring a swift end to a small group. While building up communities is itself a good, it is not a sufficient answer to the question of what is to be done.

This leaves "regime change," which, so far as I can tell, is an exciting phrase for the basically sane position that institutions should be reformed so they are better. This comes in various forms but, I am afraid, always runs through the boring old hurly-burly of democratic politics. (Paradigms focusing on the administrative state tend to be rather quiet about how you're going to get an executive who will cram the joint with dead-eyed and ruthless Catholic lawyers.) Nobody likes this answer, because it is slow and incremental, and our problems are imminent and severe. This, also, has always been the case. Between Constantine's conversion and the final shuttering of the Roman state cult and state-sponsored bloodsport, a moral horror comparable to the American abortion regime, more than a century of doubtlessly tedious institution-building and politicking passed — and the final blow was still so precipitous that Theodosius II faced near-revolution at court.

While I am less persuaded of (or invested in) the Declaration's status as revealed scripture or a perfect articulation of whatever flavor of natural law theory is in vogue at Princeton this week, the American experiment continues to give Catholics useful tools, particularly relative to those on offer from the more militant strains of American liberalism that wish to do away with or eschatologize that experiment. The freedoms of speech, religion, and association remain invaluable for any minority group that wishes to organize and effect policy. And, thanks to whatever strange providence governs our affairs, America remains significantly less demoralized than every other developed Christian nation, not an insignificant asset. (Contrast Italy, with its three-quarters Catholic population, abysmal churchgoing rates, and ongoing voluntary extinction.)

Despite mass disaffiliation from religion, the Church in America is still relatively large, well-coordinated, and wealthy, although she will probably have to sell a lot of real estate in the near term. Catholics must be willing to act as a bloc, however, and that demands better formation than has been seen on these shores in at least a century. The failure of Catholic education has been the failure of the Church in America; it is evident in our churchgoing numbers, and it is evident in the quality of our hierarchs.

Yet we have been given a second chance. The COVID crisis revealed the public schools' rot and sent parents seeking alternatives. The current administration has shown an appetite for clearing regulation and helping the school-choice movement. A statesmanlike bishop (or bishops' conference) would devote himself to a well-capitalized, high-quality parochial school system. Only thus will the Church form Catholic citizens, the first necessary condition for accomplishing anything else.

Take, as an example, the Archdiocese of Baltimore, the United States' primatial see. Within Baltimore's city limits, about two thousand people are in the pews on any given Sunday. The capacity is forty-five thousand. The situation in the suburbs is less grim, but only marginally so; attendance never bounced back after the COVID pandemic. The chronic shortage of diocesan priests has started the wheels of parish consolidation rolling anyway. Simply put, there are no congregations and no priests to serve them. What's the point of holding on to churches for them to sit empty? Granted, Baltimore's real-estate market is depressed relative to its surroundings, but it defies belief that there are not some millions to be made by turning these plum properties over to developers. (Of course, some clever maneuvering would be required at just this moment to avoid the lamentable depredations of bankruptcy court, as the archdiocese finishes paying the dues for its part in the wickedness of the sexual abuse scandal.) Sad, yes, but probably inevitable. Will the proceeds go toward the future, or will they sit and gather interest as congregations continue to dwindle on the model of the Christian Scientists or the Swedenborgians — well-endowed sects with virtually no adherents?

Reviving Catholic education will be expensive. High-quality lay teachers are expensive. In Maryland, the average teacher's salary is in the ballpark of $80,000. Catholic schools must be actually competitive on salary; the Church's consistent expectation that her lay employees will sacrifice their own interests and those of their families does nothing but breed resentment among the better teachers and attract mediocrities who cannot hack it in the public schools. Until the teaching orders recover — an iffy piece of optimism — talent will cost money.

Similarly, Catholic schools must be competitive on tuition. To make them free may not be viable, but the expense of Catholic education regularly cuts out the most loyal lay Catholics — those who actually have large families.

What would a good Catholic school system look like? An insightful article by Nathan Payne at *The Lamp* lays out what it should *not* be:

> In my experience, diocesan Catholic schools single-mindedly focus on meeting the benchmarks for renewed accreditation, perhaps even more than they attend to increasing enrollment, though that concern is a close second. In focusing on these concerns, schools ignore Our Lord's great principle: "Seek ye first the kingdom of God and his righteousness, and all these things shall be added unto you."[1]

That is to say, the practitioners of "educational science" must be kept far from the reins of power in this embryonic system. Let any staffer who utters a variant of the phrase "technology in the classroom" be cast down from the roof of a very high building. Catholic schools as they exist tend to chase fads to "keep up" with public education. Yet the very opportunity afforded us has as its premise that the public schools are in large part wretched and actually opposed to the end of education, and in almost every instance literally opposed to the goal of catechesis.

These schools must be good schools — they will have to compete with their secular peers — but they must also be, above all, catechetically sound, or the whole effort will be for nought. The rigorous but irreligious Jesuit high school

---

[1] Nathan Payne, "Why Catholics Can't Read," *The Lamp* Issue 25, Christ the King 2024.

that inevitably haunts every diocese is emphatically *not* helping to form Catholics, to build the sort of bloc we are here proposing.

None of this is easy. Yet it is necessary. The ship of the American Church is sinking. Are we going to roll a fresh coat of paint onto the decks, awaiting our inevitable inundation in more or less acceptable style, or are we going to pour our every resource into making sure the lifeboats are sound?

Of course, the program outlined in extreme brevity here works only if the hierarchy, from the episcopal cathedra on down, is committed to the project. That itself may be difficult; the American Church is chockful of the castoffs of the MBA class, bottom-line men whose interest is to make the decline as gentle and genteel as possible. Yet surely, even among these, the prospect of extinction will inspire some.

There is no hope for Catholics in political life, American or otherwise; hope does not reside in president, prince, or pasha, but in the Cross of Jesus Christ. Yet we can — and must — work to make things a little better on this mortal coil.

∞ ∞ ∞

JUDE RUSSO *is the managing editor of* The American Conservative.

14

Building a Catholic Force to be Reckoned With
A Blueprint

MAREK JAN CHODAKIEWICZ

HAT IS MEANT BY "THE AMERICAN experiment": world's lifeboat? shining city on a hill? the Puritan Empire? In my reckoning, America is a fumbling giant, confused and weakened but not yet dead. The possibility of moral regeneration, of another Great Awakening, is fairly strong, but we must fight for it and bring it about without fear.

Protestant America, however, is largely dead. The WASPs surrendered in the wake of the countercultural revolution of the 1960s. A late friend, Faith Ryan Whittlesey, a Reagan stalwart and twice U.S. ambassador to Switzerland, used to tell me in disgust, "We WASPs do not even control the membership rolls of the West Palm Beach Tennis Club anymore." Whittlesey converted to Catholicism. There certainly was a Catholic moment in America in the 1950s; it showed great promise, only to peter out for lack of zeal and strategy.

Our American system, the liberal dictatorship of pleasure, makes it extremely difficult to foster martyrs. Instead, it mass produces softies, or outright hedonists, who wouldn't be caught dead shouting *¡Viva Cristo Rey!* Some will shrug and ask: In our liberal context, how effective would that be? The answer depends on how strong our faith and will are. We must rejuvenate our faith and apply our iron will to the *Reconquista* of the American project. Retaking America from the left-liberal armies must start with faith and culture. The American project needs rejuvenation, not resuscitation.

Catholics should not expect a "place at the table." We should build our own table, and others will come, and still others will be invited when we are ready. Jesus preached that His Kingdom is not of this world, so we shall not build an earthly Jerusalem. We are also supposed to fight the good fight; therefore, we should get organized. We should keep tabs on the political system and, most of all, the culture. This entails fielding our own candidates, or making demands of those who seek our votes, establishing criteria for our support. We must rewrite the *Index of Forbidden Books*, adding to it movies, websites, podcasts, and the like. Boycotts must be in the cards: from pickets to cyber counteroffensives. A Catholic force empowered by strategically developed activism will be invited to the mainstream table sooner or later, if only to placate us. And we'll have to make a choice whether to accept the invitation. Perhaps some should, to appear accommodating and tolerant, while others should persist in various forms of civil disobedience.

As for how Catholics ought to "intervene directly in the political structuring and organization of social life" in America, there must be a multidimensional approach. Each option will address a different aspect of the good fight, and all options must complement the others. The objective is victory over the totalitarians (not authoritarians). There should be a division of labor in congruence with temper and character. Some are ready to be *Militia Christi*; others are much less hardcore. We must figure out the question of discipline and hierarchy. There must be coordination between the factions, with a discrete coordinating leadership operating a liaison network.

Some Catholic activists will be poster children for toleration and accommodation. They will be delegated to deal with the aggressor directly. They will turn the other cheek and publicly indulge humiliation. This will trigger

sympathy for our cause. Meanwhile, other Catholics will
resist, either actively or passively, generally or particularly.
For example, there is already a strong pro-life movement;
some participants have gone to prison, others are willing
to go to prison for their beliefs. The movement's various
strains must be encouraged to amplify their particular
narratives: from soft and moderate to hardcore and uncompromising. The trick will be to keep everyone together,
while we work separately for the same end goal.

Is there hope? Yes. Hope springs eternal and is the
mainspring of our faith. Self-ghettoizing facilitates further
marginalization and irrelevance. The times call for giving
witness. Naturally, this does not preclude (and, in fact,
calls for) building a robust Catholic life via a network of
parishes, churches, schools, and other institutions that
feed resources and volunteers into the multiple projects
of resistance.

But make no a mistake: The so-called Benedict Option
is not enough. The secret police will knock on our doors,
no matter how strong our resistance network is. I know
whereof I speak. I grew up in Poland in the 1960s and 1970s.
My parents were anti-communists, Catholic human-rights
activists. Both were arrested. My paternal grandmother
survived the Gestapo, NKVD, and Polish Communist
secret police. Her husband survived the Gulag. The Soviets
tried to kidnap my father as a "Soviet orphan," but his
grandfather saved him by fleeing what suddenly became
the USSR. Later, my father was arrested for his dissident
activities and served time in jail in Poland. My mother was
first detained by the communists when she was five, along
with her eight-year-old brother. The secret police seized
their parents and sent the whole family to prison.

I could multiply the stories of horror and persecution
by both Nazis and communists, *enemigos de nuestro Señor
Jesucristo*. But enough. What we need are more symposia like this to work out strategy, operations, and tactics
of the vanguard and then massive Catholic resistance

(networking with our evangelical brethren who will also be martyrs).

Finally, let us not forget our allies among the godly of other faiths. No one "owns the libs" online better than the Libs of TikTok, an account on X run by an Orthodox Jewess. There are many more like her who adhere to Judaism. Also, Muslim parents were the ones who openly fought against the transgender threats to their kids in Maryland, demanding the government leave them alone. Christians, including Catholics, failed to coalesce in this resistance as a bloc. Let's take care of secularism before we can remind everyone that *Extra Ecclesiam nulla salus*.

This symposium is a good beginning. We shall see what follows.

∞ ∞ ∞

MAREK JAN CHODAKIEWICZ *is a professor of history at the Institute of World Politics: A Graduate School of National Security and International Affairs in Washington, D.C. He holds the Tadeusz Kosciuszko Chair of Polish Studies and heads the Center for Intermarium Studies.*

15

Catholic Organization:

A Universal Vision of Both Word and Deed

CHRISTOPHER ZEHNDER

WHEN ASKED, "IS THE AMERICAN experiment an exhausted project?" we may answer with a question: "The American experiment in what?" If it is an experiment "in representational government," or in democracy, it is hardly specifically American. If it is an experiment because of what it proposes as the end or purpose of government and the state, and if that purpose differs radically from that proposed by the Catholic political tradition, we should hope the American experiment is an "exhausted project." If it is, again, an experiment in representational government, the American experiment is unobjectionable; the popular are among the valid forms of government, and where they are customary, they should (all things being equal) be preserved. But where all things are not equal—where, for instance, the people can or will no longer act the part of citizens—we find not only exhaustion but decay. In such cases, the forms of representational government continue on merely as forms; without the invigoration of the citizen's sense of responsibility, they become a means of imposing a demagogic and oligarchic agenda. That seems to be the state of things today for various reasons, not least of which is the playing out of the proposal of the ends of government by the American founding itself and the Enlightenment tradition of which it was, in part at least, an expression. This proposal I call America's "civic religion."

Historically, the Catholic's "place at the table" in the United States has always been conditioned on his acceptance of, or at least acquiescence to, this "civic religion." In its best formulation, this "religion" confesses that the highest purpose of civic life is temporal human happiness, which is to be realized in part through a public order founded on justice. I say "in part" because for the American civic religion, the pursuit of happiness is finally an individual endeavor the ends and means of which are to be determined by each person. At least for an historically influential strain of American thought, virtue plays a role in directing individual endeavor, but only as an instrumental good — it conduces to happiness; it is its necessary context, but it does not constitute happiness. Likewise, religion. American founders such as George Washington praised religion, but in language that suggests its value rests in inculcating virtue, seen as an essential underpinning and support of a republican social order. Whatever else religion is beyond that is abandoned to the private sphere to determine.

For the Catholic, virtue is not simply a means of securing happiness; it is happiness. Virtue encompasses the moral "cardinal" virtues (justice, temperance, prudence, and fortitude) and virtues of the intellect (knowledge of the truth, understanding, and wisdom). Virtue thus understood is perfected and elevated by the theological virtues (faith, hope, and charity), through which men attain their end or purpose: *theosis,* union with God, "becoming God." It is only thus that we are made happy with the happiness that is integral to our nature. As the happiness toward which we strive, in the possession of which we are blessed, virtue is the highest expression of the common good — the good that society and the state exist to protect and foster.

Such an understanding of the state has always been foreign to the American mind; hence, the Catholic's difficulty in finding his place "at the table." Nevertheless, historically, a general Christian sense in American society made it possible for Catholics to participate in the political order; bigotry mostly, not principle, stood in his way. In the current, postmodern atmosphere, where the appeal to truth is seen as merely a play for power, principle has made it harder for Catholics to play a part in the political order, especially as elected officials. For instance, a candidate who is fully Catholic would find it hard to be elected if he voiced support for a living wage while opposing abortion — he would alienate each side of the political spectrum. And he would alienate both sides together if he voiced any opposition to, supported restrictions on, or just opposed public funding for *in vitro* fertilization. The incomprehension that would meet his position would likely cost him the election.

Nevertheless, even today, avenues do exist by which Catholics may influence American society, and they are as multiple as the conditions of Catholic life in our time. They may take the "Benedictine" model of intentional Catholic community building, what would provide models of Christian social life beyond the nuclear family. They may be more Dominican — living in the context of the world, passing on the fruit of one's contemplation. They may be Franciscan with the embrace of a voluntary "poverty" that witnesses to the simplicity of life and abnegation that are the soil in which virtue thrives. In a word, Catholics may influence American society by evangelizing it both by word and example.

Such evangelization includes preaching the Gospel, as well as "pre-evangelization" — preparing the ground in which the seed of the Word can take root. We till this field — which is political in the fullest sense — by recalling our neighbors and fellow citizens to a renewed understanding of natural truths about the cosmos, man himself, and human community in all its aspects — familial, economic, cultural, and political. To accomplish this, we may form specifically Catholic groups or organizations dedicated to the full expression of Catholic social teaching. So organized, we may enter into temporary alliances with non-Catholic, even non-Christian, organizations in the pursuit of limited goals, such as campaigns for the defense of human life, for economic justice, to protect the integrity of creation, and to oppose the injustice of war. Such groups would allow an unadulterated Catholic voice to address the issues of our time while not losing the effective interaction, support, and friendship of other men of good will.

The ready models our society offers for the Catholic group or groups that I propose are of two kinds: activist and intellectual. The activist engages society directly through advocacy, intervention, and service. The intellectual promotes ideas by argumentation, scholarship, and debate — think "think tanks" or journals. What I propose is a Catholic organization or organizations that would unite both functions — to keep the thinkers from running off into abstractions and the doers from floating rudderless in a sea of seemingly unrelated particulars. Our Catholic organizations would be political in the broader sense by addressing the life of the polis; they would not be partisan or run candidates for public office. Rather, being Catholic, they would strive to rise above party ambition and squabble to delineate a universal vision by both word and deed.

In its activism, a group of this sort would engage existential injustices in the light of Catholic teaching, joining with other groups to achieve particular ends. In so doing, it need only address and advocate the measures to be promoted; its task would not be to explain them in light of the principles of Catholic teaching. Appeals to concepts of justice would be necessary, but they may be such as American society already embraces or could immediately understand; the activist's task is not to teach but to achieve. He witnesses to Catholic social teaching more by what he does, less by what he says. When Catholic advocacy transcends our country's political and social divisions, it hints at the transcendence and fullness of the Catholic worldview — its unpredictability in the eyes of those who embrace America's civic religion. The very queerness of acting Catholic politically will doubtless spark curiosity and the question, "Why?"

It is to answer "Why?" that our group engages its intellectual component. Those who make up this cohort must needs be students of Catholic social teaching in all its fullness, as expressed across the ages, from the time of the Apostles to today. In questions touching on the nature of human society, such as its governance in relation to the Church, political economy, international relations, human stewardship of creation, justice commutative and distributive, the defense of life in the womb and on the street, and war, the teachers will be the Scriptures, the Church Fathers and Doctors, the great philosophers and theologians, and especially the papal social encyclicals and the Councils (including the Second Vatican). The task will be to attempt to understand and address all social questions by transcending the facile left-right dichotomies of our day, rooted in a failed liberalism, and view them from the vantage point of eternity. Our intellectuals must pass on the fruits of their contemplation and their application to the needs of our day through every available means — to their neighbors and fellow citizens and, ultimately, the world. For wisdom is a common good that recognizes no national boundary. It belongs to all mankind.

Most importantly, the task I outline here must be carried out in the peace and love of Christ, with honor paid to the image of God in each man and woman — the root of their just human freedom and fundamental dignity. We must propose, not impose. Any proposal that would involve overturning our institutions and imposing a Catholic order by force is, at best, illusory. At worst, it would corrupt our cause, for it would involve acts of violence that we will scarcely be able to avoid and so conduce to the scandal and downfall of countless souls, not the least our own. Our only path forward is through a personal dedication to holiness and a commitment to example, proposal, and persuasion — and, if necessary, martyrdom. If our cause is to be sealed with blood, let it be our own, not our neighbor's.

∞ ∞ ∞

CHRISTOPHER ZEHNDER *is the general editor of the Catholic Textbook Project and has written four of the books in its history series. He is currently editing a history of Christendom (for which he is one of the writers) from the ancient world to the fourteenth century. He is the author of a trilogy of novels,* A Song for Else, *a story of the early, formative years of the Reformation in Germany. It is published by Arouca Press. Mr. Zehnder and his wife are lay members of the Order of Preachers (Dominicans). He is a councilman for the incorporated village of Hartford, Ohio (pop. 404).*

16

Pipedreaming about Political Power Plays

JOHN M. GRONDELSKI

ET ME BE FRANK ABOUT CATHO-lics' place in American politics: We punch below our weight, and in many ways that's our fault. Before we get into pipedreams about fundamental reconstructions of the political order, let's recognize why we punch below our political weight. Catholic political impotence is one of the corruptions *Roe v. Wade* unleashed on America. If the Catholic response to the nationwide legalization of abortion had been managed properly, we would not be in this situation.

The Church is not, of course, a political entity, but her teachings have political consequences, and she exists in a political world. The Church in the United States, however, has not reckoned with these facts. Cowed by the Johnson Amendment (1954), the Church has retreated from effective politics for fear of losing her tax-exempt status. The amendment gagged religious participation in politics because Lyndon Johnson wanted to quiet down some of his political opponents. Getting rid of that gag order is almost three-quarters of a century overdue. Why have we not demanded our ability to speak to the world without threat?

Catholic political naïveté is sometimes stunning. Two examples will suffice. First, take the March for Life. I've been part of that noble effort since the 1970s. Nellie Gray, its founder, insisted that when marchers arrive at the Capitol, they go into the Senate and House office buildings to register their presence with their two senators and representative. I don't see that so much anymore; people reach the Supreme Court building and peter off, arguably not making as deep an impression as they could.

Second, though demonstrations are important, there's something of a Mr.-Smith-goes-to-Washington approach to our political lobbying. Compare that to the culture of death, which is acutely aware of the many levers of influence and action in lawmaking. We should, but don't, match that footprint, even though Catholics make up one-quarter of the American body politic. Why not? Because our actions (and the funding that should support those actions) don't match our rhetoric. The adage says you put your money where your mouth is. We don't.

For that, the U.S. bishops bear no small responsibility. Despite Vatican II's calling abortion an "unspeakable crime," have the bishops *acted* in ways consistent with that statement? After fifty years they have yet to conduct a national pro-life collection! Of course, they can't give money to political-action groups, but they *can* support educational programs, and they *can* support crisis pregnancy centers, which, in the post-*Dobbs* era, are needed more than ever and are under increasing assault.

Part of the problem is that episcopal mouths are divided. While some bishops speak of abortion as a "paramount issue," others undermine their brothers with qualifying, temporizing, or equivocating statements of their own, at times defining "life issues" as broadly — and, thus, as meaninglessly — as possible.

There is also a group of "professional Catholics" who have never been comfortable with the pro-life movement because it's a burr to their otherwise comfortable relations with the left wing of American politics. This cabal tends to get organized — more so than the Catholic mainstream — around the time of presidential elections. With connections to Catholic academe, it manages to give cover to pro-abortion candidates. Catholics for Kamala is a case in point, as were Massimo Faggioli's paeans to Joe Biden's

Catholicism in *America* magazine and in book form. The bishops, like Charlie Brown kicking Lucy's football, fall for it every four years.

Absent *real* political organizing, it's risible to talk about transforming the political order. Reconsidering the philosophical bases of the American founding, experimenting with "integralism" or some other wholly new vision of political philosophy seems an audacious venture given our less-than-stellar performance in the existing political order. Let's be honest: If sixty million adherents can't pull off a basic and effective political lobby *within* that order, talk about reconstructing its foundations will go nowhere. For the latter to work would require a critical mass of Catholics to appreciate the philosophical and theological anthropology underlying Catholic social thought, as well as how that vision of man *qua* social animal differs in key respects from the social contractarian vision of man that undergirds "private autonomous individualism." Such an understanding is unlikely, given the general catechetical illiteracy in Catholic circles. Most Catholics would be as stumped as Ketanji Brown Jackson when asked, "What is a woman?" In other words, to pull off such a feat of reconstruction requires a critical mass that does not exist. Shouldn't we try to build it?

∞ ∞ ∞

JOHN M. GRONDELSKI *(Ph.D., Fordham) is a former associate dean of the School of Theology at Seton Hall University in South Orange, New Jersey. All views expressed herein are exclusively his.*

17

Living the Gospel in a Milieu of Arrogant Secularism

JAMES G. HANINK

S THE AMERICAN EXPERIMENT AN exhausted project? If we are to reflect on the broad American experiment, we should ask *which* Americans and *whose* experiment? For indigenous people, there was no novel experiment. There was, instead, a familiar and daunting struggle. Marked by intertribal violence and intensified by European settlement, the struggle was to defend tribal territories and sustain kinship groups. That struggle, often futile, continues. The current proliferation of gambling casinos is a sorry mockery of it.

For most European immigrants, in contrast, the overriding experiment was to remake their lives on a distant and largely unknown continent. For these immigrants, achieving economic stability was a primary goal. So, too, was keeping alive the heritage that they brought with them. Some of these newcomers also cared deeply about the freedom to practice their own religion. Among them, some few entertained as an ideal the freedom of religion for all. With the attenuation of religious practice and the rise of secularism, that ideal is increasingly in jeopardy.

For the well-established and prosperous founders, with their English background, the American experiment took the form of a provocative Constitution. Though flawed, it was a novel document that blended classical themes, Enlightenment aspirations, and Christian imperatives. Nonetheless, even the founders quickly recognized that their new Constitution required amendments. Not surprisingly, it has continued to do so. *That* continuing experiment, initiated with the Declaration of Independence, is surely not exhausted. It remains an enduring, if imperfect, achievement of self-governance. Yet, in itself, it is by no means an experiment that is enough for our flourishing now or in the decades to come. The Mandates of Democracy, as our chastened experience teaches, are only paper pledges without the people's reflective practice of civic virtues.

Can Catholics realistically expect a place at the table of American politics? Here we must first ask *which* Catholics? Duly enculturated Catholics whose frame of reference is either the exaggerated political liberalism or the distorted political conservatism of recent decades will be shown a "place at the table" of American politics. So, too, will those who cheer on an aggressive self-aggrandizing presidency. Why would we suppose otherwise? Many of their hosts are Catholics of the same compromised sort. But Catholics who understand and honor the Church's living *magisterium* cannot expect to find a seat at that table. Nor, indeed, can *anyone* who believes that it is always wrong intentionally to kill the innocent or to threaten to so act. Again, why suppose otherwise? American politics has capitulated to the now entrenched policy of nuclear deterrence, that is, the threat to use weapons of mass destruction. The costly "upgrading" of that policy comes at the special expense of the poor. American politics, in addition, has acquiesced to the increasingly widespread practice of abortion and euthanasia. This double betrayal of human life, both at its beginning and its end, is starkly incompatible with the inherent dignity of humankind. It is a betrayal that the politics of domination accelerates.

What is the best way for Catholics to intervene directly in the political structuring and organization of social life in America? Living the Gospel, day in and day out, is the only credible way of preaching the Gospel. In living the Gospel, we help shape both our politics and our culture; each in turn informs the other. At their best, Catholic parishes already form small, local, and intentional communities. For these parishes to succeed, they need to promote schools and social services grounded in the faith. They also need to foster the Catholic professional groups and labor organizations to which their parishioners belong. Doing so depends on the cooperation of their sponsoring dioceses.

Insofar as fresh endeavors akin to the Benedict Option act in harmony with local parishes and their dioceses, they can enhance what is already in place. Indeed, they can become catalysts of renewal. In this ongoing dynamic, authentic reform reflects the dictum of St. Ignatius of Antioch: where the bishop is, there is the Church.

Living the Gospel, the animating source of Catholic social teaching, brings center stage the common good, the *telos* of political and social life. Unlike the utilitarian chimera of the greatest good for the greatest number, the common good embraces the good of all. In advancing the common good, the principles of solidarity, subsidiarity, and economic democracy come into play.

Solidarity, with its spirit of one for all and all for one, insists that the first measure of justice is how we treat the most vulnerable. It recognizes that vulnerability is embedded in the human condition. Subsidiarity tells us that we best realize our civic potential when we act in a decentralized and calibrated way. It understands that civic character stems from the active engagement of citizens, an engagement that unchecked centralization undermines. Economic democracy calls for an increasingly widespread distribution of goods and resources. Effective distribution leads to an ownership society. Without economic democracy, political democracy is illusory. If only the rich, or those with the backing of the rich, can effectively seek public office, political democracy perishes.

Today, only the fledgling American Solidarity Party embraces the principles of solidarity, subsidiarity, and economic democracy. It understands, moreover, that the principle of solidarity works in harmony with a consistent ethic of life. The ASP is so at odds with, and contrary to, the political establishments of "right" and "left" that it faces the sharp opposition of both in its struggle to gain ballot access.

Integralism, as now discussed, is simply wrongheaded. The state, unless it sheds the pretense of absolute sovereignty and checks the soft tyranny of bureaucracy, makes for a dismal collaborator. Nor should the Church seek to exercise coercive power. Doing so contravenes the Gospel and historically has led to grave wrongs.

Is there any hope for Catholics in American political life? *Dum spiro, spero!* So wrote Cicero, believing that while we breathe there is hope. Unlike a geometrical abstraction, our political life is a contingently shifting phenomenon. Its very nature is changeable; over the past century, it has often and dramatically changed. Throughout the past century, it has included a wide range of competing tendencies.

For starters, consider our conflicted record of nationalism and internationalism, of individualism and tribalism, of imperialism and retrenchment. Consider, too, the intermingling of seemingly incompatible perspectives. One telling example of this phenomenon is a serpentine populism that sheds one skin and posthaste takes on another. The upshot is that one pundit's populism is another pundit's mob rule.

The passing parade of political life, to our entertainment, has featured an often surprising and larger-than-life cast of characters. Among them we find the visionary FDR and the likeable General Dwight D. Eisenhower, the Kennedys of Camelot, an angry George Wallace and a wily Lyndon B. Johnson, a peanut farmer named Jimmy, the millionaire Bushes, and now a rampaging wheeler-dealer dubbed "the Donald." In recent times, before our eyes, our chaotic and monetized political life has reflected and, in turn, promoted an arrogant secularism. But history shows that no regime can maintain itself indefinitely. The politics of power is ultimately self-destructive.

Politically engaged and faithful Catholics — would that they were a legion rather than a remnant — surely do have hope. But we need to reject the constricting binaries of left and right, of liberal and conservative. Instead, we need to search out common ground to advance the common good. In doing so, let us remember that unless the Lord build the city, they labor in vain who build. Allow me to conclude my reflection with a proposal made in hope: Let us adopt the motto of St. Junípero Serra, to which he held fast as he literally limped along the whole coast of California: *Siempre adelante, con juicio* . . . Always forward, with judgment.

∞ ∞ ∞

JAMES G. HANINK, *a contributing editor of the* New Oxford Review, *is an independent scholar, though more independent than scholarly!*

18

Integralism:

A Non-Individualistic Understanding of Human Life

EDMUND WALDSTEIN, O.CIST.

THE AMERICAN EXPERIMENT OF A republican government without an established religion was a key step in the transition to the modern world. While elements of the American experiment drew on the wisdom of the ancients, there were also distinctly modern elements that would be copied and radicalized in other parts of the world, as modern civilization was formed. To ask what role Catholics ought to play in American politics is thus, in part, to ask how Catholics ought to position themselves toward modernity.

One way of examining this question is by looking at different ways of interpreting the encyclical letter *Longinqua oceani* that Pope Leo XIII sent to the to the bishops of the United States in 1895. Pope Leo begins by recalling that the Catholic hierarchy was established in America at the time when the thirteen colonies (with the help of Catholic France) won independence from Britain and takes the occasion of praising "the great Washington," for understanding that "without morality the *res publica* cannot endure."[1] The Church being the restorer and preserver of morality, Americans ought to welcome her influence, as giving support to her temporal common good (even apart from the supernatural good that she brings).[2]

Pope Leo goes on to praise the "equity of the laws" of

---

[1] Pope Leo XIII, *Longinqua oceani* (1895), §4.
[2] Ibid.

the "well-ordered Republic" of America, which gives the Church a liberty that enabled her rapid growth in the preceding century.[3] Nevertheless, he warns that that one ought not to conclude from this that the American model of Church-state relations is the exemplar that should be followed in all cases:

> [It] would be very erroneous to draw the conclusion that in America is to be sought the type of the most desirable status of the Church, or that it would be universally lawful or expedient for State and Church to be, as in America, dissevered and divorced. The fact that Catholicity with you is in good condition, nay, is even enjoying a prosperous growth, is by all means to be attributed to the fecundity with which God has endowed His Church, in virtue of which, unless men or circumstances interfere, she spontaneously expands and propagates herself; but she would bring forth more abundant fruits if, in addition to liberty, she enjoyed the favor of the laws and the patronage of the public authority.[4]

The background of this warning is Leo's worries about France. Certain French Catholics saw in America an alternative version of the separation of Church and state, one that was not hostile to the Church (as French laicism was). But Leo was hoping for the reestablishment of a fully Catholic political order in France (through democratic means), and therefore, while recognizing that the American order was better than the hostile separation pursued by French liberals, he continued to stress that it was not the ideal.

There are two ways of reading Pope Leo XIII's teaching in this encyclical. The first sees it as a tentative step on the path of the Church's full acceptance of modernity, a step that goes in the right direction but has, in certain respects, been superseded by subsequent steps. The second sees it

---

[3] Ibid., §6.
[4] Ibid.

as a teaching of a permanent principle that can never be
superseded.

The view that sees *Longinqua oceani* as a step in the
Church's path to accepting the achievements of modernity typically portrays Leo as having understood that the
absolute and unqualified rejection of modernity proposed
by Popes such as Gregory XVI and Pius IX, as well as the
defense of the *ancien régime* mounted by Catholic reac-
tionaries and Romantics such as Joseph de Maistre and
Louis de Bonald,[5] must be rejected as dead ends, tying
the Church too closely to a defective political order — the
absolutist monarchical order of the seventeenth and eigh-
teenth centuries. Hence, he called for a revival of Thomism,
a philosophy that understood the principles of ancient and
medieval "mixed" regimes — republics with monarchical
and aristocratic as well as democratic elements. This philosophy would enable a *rapprochement* with what was good
about modernity, while continuing to reject the aggressively
secularist and relativistic aspects of modern philosophy.
Hence Leo's praise of America in *Longinqua oceani,* and
his policy of *Ralliement* in France, which urged French
Catholics to give up intransigent monarchism for a participation in French republican political life. Nevertheless,
so this account continues, Leo was still hampered by an
outdated view of the desirability of an explicit recognition
of the Catholic Church and her authority by the state. It
was not until Vatican II that the Church completed the
path that Leo had begun, recognizing the legitimate "auton-
omy of earthly affairs"[6] and, in the declaration *Dignitatis
humanae,* the right of religious liberty, founded on the
dignity of the human person, which excludes the kind of
Catholic political order after which Leo had still yearned.

---

[5] For a typical expression of this widespread view see: George Wei-
gel, "Ironies in the Fire: Catholicism and Modernity," Fifth Annual
Edward Cardinal Egan Lecture, Magnificat Foundation, Union
League Club of New York City (April 29, 2017), eppc.org/publication/
ironies-in-the-fire-catholicism-and-modernity.

[6] *Gaudium et spes* (1965), §36.

My own view of *Longingqua oceani* is different. While I agree with the forgoing account up to a point — Leo was indeed moving beyond the reactionary Romanticism of the likes of de Maistre to a deeper understanding of politics drawn from St. Thomas — I disagree with the thesis that his teaching on Church-state relations has been superseded by Vatican II. I believe that *Dignitatis humanae*'s insistence that it "leaves untouched traditional Catholic doctrine on the moral duty of men and societies toward the true religion and toward the one Church of Christ"[7] should be taken seriously. Leo XIII's qualified judgment about the American order is therefore still valid today. While the liberty of the Church affirmed by the American founding documents is indeed superior to the sort of hostile separation of Church and state found in France, it is not the ideal, since it does not fully realize the social duties of human beings toward the one Church of Christ.

To my critics, such "integralism" seems a hopeless dead end, an attempt to tie Catholics to superseded elements of the Leonine teaching and hampering a truly fruitful and creative engagement with contemporary political reality. Today's integralists, they suggest, are hindering the implementation of the teachings of Vatican II and the postconciliar popes, just as intransigent French monarchists hampered the implementation of Leo's *Ralliement*. But to my mind, integralism is both necessary and fruitful for Catholic engagement in American political life.

The key principle behind Leo's teaching is a non-individualistic understanding of human life and the human good. This non-individualistic understanding has deep roots both in classical philosophy and in Scripture itself. Aristotle had seen that human beings are political animals — their perfection can only be found in a shared civic life of virtue, in the pursuit of common goods greater than themselves. And Scripture confirms this insight, deepening it through revealed teaching. The Book of Revelation, for

---

[7] *Dignitatis humanae* (1965), §1.

example, portrays the Heavenly City not only as fulfilling all the messianic prophecies given to Israel but also as the fulfillment of the political hopes of the Gentiles themselves. St. John was aware that many of his readers in the Greek-speaking cities of Asia Minor were torn between their desire to participate in the civic life of their own cities, the arena of human perfection, and their desire to participate in the new life of Christ. He therefore shows them that the truest civic life was only possible in the City of God.[8] It is this non-individualistic understanding of human life and politics upon which Leo bases his teaching on the duties of human political societies to recognize the true faith. In *Immortale Dei*, Leo argues that societies are just as bound to serve God in truth as individuals are, and that the civil authority is therefore bound to recognize and favor the true religion.[9]

Where does this leave Catholics with respect to America today? There is little short-term prospect of establishing the "thesis" of an integrally Catholic state; therefore it seems they must accept the "hypothesis" of a pluralistic political community with liberty for the Church.[10] I believe that integralism is helpful to Catholics in American political life in several ways.

First, it should help them in their own reading of the American tradition. As I hinted above, the American founding is complex.[11] One strand in the American founding is based on the individualistic political philosophy of John Locke. This strand sees politics as ordered to the defense of subjective individual rights, that is, the liberty of each

---

[8] Cf. My paper "Politics as a Sketch for the Church," *New Polity* Issue 2.1 (Feb. 2021), pp. 6–32, at 8–9.

[9] Pope Leo XIII, *Immortale Dei* (1885), §6.

[10] For the thesis/hypothesis distinction see: Maurice Bévenot, S.J., "Thesis and Hypothesis," *Theological Studies* 15.3 (1954), pp. 440–446.

[11] For the following see my article: "Hard Liberalism, Soft Liberalism, and the American Founding," *Integralism and the Common Good: Selected Essays from the Josias*, Volume 1: *Family, City, and State*, ed. P. Edmund Waldstein, O.Cist., and Peter A. Kwasniewski (Brooklyn, NY: Angelico Press, 2021), pp. 286–305.

to seek individual goals without being interfered with by government. But there is another strand in the American founding based on classical republicanism (especially on Cicero, and through him on Aristotle), which sees the public good as the goal of politics. As Matthew J. Peterson has shown, most of the founders combined both strands, seeing the aim of government as being *both* the defense of individual rights *and* the public good.[12] Peterson argues that these things go together; the defense of individual rights makes an integral contribution to the common good, even though the common good goes beyond them. Did the founders see the public good as ordered to individual rights, or individual rights to the public good? Peterson reads at least some of them as subordinating individual rights to the common good. I believe that Catholic Americans should adopt something like this reading of the American tradition, emphasizing the elements drawn from Cicero, Aristotle, and the Bible, and de-emphasizing the Lockean element.

Second, integralism helps Catholics to see that political societies will not in fact be neutral about ultimate questions. The modern split between "the state" as a neutral referee and "civil society" as the arena of debate about human ends, does not fit with the political nature of human beings. In fact, all states will act on the basis of an understanding of the human good, whether explicitly or implicitly. Catholics ought therefore to combat the stealth establishment of the religion of postmodern liberalism and replace it with an orientation toward the real goods of human life. Both in law and in politics they ought to frankly pursue a substantive notion of the common good. They should therefore welcome developments such as the "common good constitutionalism" of Adrian Vermeule, which

> sees that law is parental, a wise teacher and an inculcator of good habits. Just authority in rulers

---

[12] Matthew J. Peterson, "The Meaning of the Public Good in the Rhetoric of Ratification," (dissertation, Claremont Graduate University, 2013).

> can be exercised for the good of subjects, if nec-
> essary even against the subjects' own perceptions
> of what is best for them — perceptions that may
> change over time anyway, as the law teaches, habit-
> uates, and re-forms them.[13]

They should also welcome certain aspects of the vision of politicians such as J. D. Vance, who argued in 2021 that government should "reward the things that we think are good" and "punish the things that we think are bad."[14] While I do not agree with all of Vance's policies, I think his ascent to the vice-presidency is a hopeful sign for Catholic engagement in American political life.

In the long term, however, I think we should not be too certain that the "thesis" of integrally Catholic political societies will never return. The future is always uncertain. Political orders can rise and fall and be transformed in the most unexpected and even rapid fashion. The political conclusions that follow from the truth can reemerge in surprising ways. Which Christian during the persecution of Diocletian would have predicted the rise of Constantine and Theodosius?

∞ ∞ ∞

EDMUND WALDSTEIN, O. Cist., *is a monk of Stift Heiligen-kreuz in Austria and a lecturer in moral theology. Born in Rome and raised in the United States and Austria, he is editor of the two-volume series* Integralism and the Common Good: Selected Essays from The Josias.

---

[13] Adrian Vermeule, "Beyond Originalism," *The Atlantic* (March 31, 2020).

[14] Cited in: Will Steakin and Katherine Faulders, "Vance argued for higher tax rate on childless Americans in 2021 interview," *ABC News* (July 6, 2024), abcnews.go.com/US/vance-argued-higher-tax-rate-child-less-americans-2021/story?id=112284318.

19

Catholic Existence in a Protestant Experiment

THOMAS STORCK

HE UNITED STATES HAS ALWAYS been a Protestant project. Whether conceived as an "experiment" or not, it traces its intellectual roots to English Protestantism, a Protestantism unable to defend itself intellectually and hence soon to be transformed by currents of Enlightenment thought. The Protestant character of this country has been noted many times, but a timely iteration of this was recently expressed by the American journalist Rod Dreher:

> I did not realize until I began traveling extensively in Europe how profoundly Protestant—and English Protestant—the United States is, that despite our superficial diversity, the American identity is built on an English Protestant conception of the world. Even our Catholics and Orthodox have been Protestantized, because they live in a Protestant nation, for better or for worse. When in earlier decades we Americans insisted that immigrants assimilate, what we expected them to assimilate to was a culture based on English Protestant values, which were the values of the country's founders. ("'Race,' 'Nation' and Modern Times," *The American Conservative* online, July 28, 2022).

First, however, I insist on a distinction: If we are Catholics who happen to live in the United States, then, in common with all Catholics anywhere, we owe our country certain obligations that come under the heading of legal

justice: to obey just laws, to pay taxes, and so on. But we
most definitely do not owe it any kind of duty to embrace
any particular philosophy, to buy into an experiment con-
trived by Enlightenment political theorists or to see our
country as something greater than what it is, one country
among many, with virtues and vices, just like any of the
common run of nations. Although history unfolds under
the providence of God, nevertheless it is wrong to see the
immense wealth and power this country presently possesses
as a sign of God's special approval. Doubtless they will in
time diminish or disappear, as they have from every other
powerful nation in the past. And we might learn from
Sacred Scripture that just because a country is large and
powerful does not mean it is especially favored or blessed
by Almighty God.

Granting, then, the duties associated with legal justice,
Catholics must figure out how to exist within this Protestant behemoth. Can we exist within a Protestant milieu
without ourselves becoming Protestant in our thinking?
Can we realize that we must seek to foster and preserve
not only Catholic doctrine but Catholic culture? Sadly, the
millions of Catholic immigrants to this country have had
no substantive effect on American culture. As the Colum-
bia University historian and Catholic convert Carlton J. H.
Hayes said in 1922 in a graduation address at the College of
New Rochelle, "In spite of the Church's amazing growth,
American Catholics have had no such influence upon the
thought and life of the whole nation as their numbers
would lead us to expect." In fact, we exist on sufferance
of the non-Catholic majority, who expect us to behave
and adapt ourselves to their ways of thinking and acting.
Usually we are only too glad to oblige.

This occurs in every area of human social life, but has
been particularly obvious in the realm of electoral politics,
as we can see from two notable historical examples. John F.
Kennedy's September 1960 speech to the Houston Minis-
terial Association both reveals a privatized understanding

of religion, a restriction of religion to the merely personal realm, subordinate to the perceived real business of life, and at the same time upholds the Protestant principle of private judgment as the basis for our decisions. Our faith, our commitment to the Church and her teaching, on this view, becomes merely a private matter, something of no importance beyond the personal. "I believe in a president whose religious views are his own private affair," Kennedy stated. And a little later, "Whatever issues may come before me as president — on birth control, divorce, censorship, gambling or any other subject — I will make my decision ... in accordance with what my conscience tells me to be the national interest."

Apparently one's "religious views" have no relationship with the business of governing. They are a "private affair" — so private, in fact, as to be harmless and ultimately meaningless. What sort of a religion is that which has no significance in making decisions on the important issues that come before any political figure? It is a mere chimera, detached from the real life of politics or business, where decisions are made with very different criteria. "I do not speak for my church on public matters, and the church does not speak for me," declared Kennedy. And truly so. Here we see not just the separation of church and state but the banishing of religion from public life, from any role except that of psychological solace or a prop to personal morality.

But, sadly, this did not begin with Kennedy. In the April 1927 *Atlantic Monthly*, a Protestant attorney, Charles Marshall, in his "Open Letter to the Honorable Alfred E. Smith," asked how Smith could reconcile the teachings of the Catholic Church with his constitutional duties were he elected president. Marshall included numerous quotes from Pius IX and Leo XIII in his article, for example, from Leo's encyclical *Immortale Dei*, "It is not lawful for the State, any more than for the individual, either to disregard all religious duties or to hold in equal favor different kinds of religion," and from his *Longinqua oceani*, "It would be very erroneous to draw the conclusion that in America is to be sought the type of the most desirable status of the Church."

Smith replied with an indignant protest in the same magazine the next month: "By what right do you ask me to assume responsibility for every statement that may be made in any encyclical letter?" And, he continued, were some law

> to be passed which violated the common morality of all God-fearing men . . . how would a Protestant resolve it? Obviously by the dictates of his conscience. That is exactly what a Catholic would do. There is no ecclesiastical tribunal which would have the slightest claim upon the obedience of Catholic communicants in the resolution of such a conflict.

Here also we find the same assertion as that made by Kennedy: My own conscience, my private judgment, not the teaching of the Church, is what would inform my decisions. What sort of religion did Smith and Kennedy adhere to, that apparently would have no influence on their activities as statesmen? One whose teachings were subordinate to the private judgment of the individual. What sort of Church did they belong to, that had nothing to say on the things that matter for the affairs of nations — or at least nothing that anyone need pay any attention to?

It should be obvious that both Smith and Kennedy saw their religion as something merely personal, divorced from the actuality of real life. "I believe in a president whose religious views are his own private affair." They both embraced the Protestant principle of private judgment as the standard for their conduct of public business. It is their personal consciences that were to determine national policy, consciences that apparently need have little or no connection with their professed religious beliefs. In both cases, these candidates were prepared to participate in the

"American experiment" on its own terms, however much that required they put aside their professed religious beliefs.

In the case of both Smith and Kennedy there was no widespread outrage on the part of their fellow Catholics on this betrayal of the faith. Their conception of the role of Catholics in the American political order was doubtless that shared by a majority of their co-religionists, a conception of politics that sets aside the Catholic faith from any important place in human affairs. But if this understanding of the relationship between religion and secular affairs is connatural to American culture, we must ask the question of how or whether the Church can be at home here.

If we look into the encyclicals of Leo XIII that deal with the political and social order, encyclicals that Al Smith considered irrelevant to his political work, we will see that as long as the Church remains true to her God-given mission of proclaiming the whole Gospel, she will never entirely fit into any cultural or political order shaped by an ethos foreign to her own. She must either convert that society or remain at the margins. For some time, Catholics have striven to fit into America, but at the cost of downplaying both Catholic doctrine and Catholic culture, pretending that we could wholeheartedly join in a common effort with those who are not of the faith. This was a mistake, a mistake that should by now be clear to everyone. But despite the obviousness of that mistake, multitudes of Catholics still appear to think that with a bit of touching up here and there, American society can be made into something Catholics can cozy up to. As long as we keep on thinking like this, we will again and again be disappointed and never succeed in our divinely given mission of converting our country and the rest of the world to the true faith.

Until recently we have had a president for four years who is juridically a Catholic. We now have a vice president likewise juridically a Catholic. Both of them publicly disagree with more than one moral teaching of the Church, and it is hard to think of *any* recent Catholic politician who

has made the faith and Catholic culture the foundation
of his worldview. At best, they have uncomfortably yoked
an opposition to abortion and suchlike evils to an otherwise essentially liberal understanding of man and society. I
cannot imagine an informed Catholic who held to all the
teachings of the Church making any headway in American
politics. Perhaps at the local level, where such matters can
often be ignored, a genuine Catholic could fulfill a limited
political role, but it is hard to see how that could be done
on the national stage or even at the state level. Too many
compromises would be required even to get elected.

What is the solution for this?

Many Catholics who take the Church's teaching on the
social order seriously have of late begun to label themselves
as integralists. That is a term I can accept for myself, so
long as we mean by it simply someone who affirms the
Church's teaching on the sociopolitical order. But if by
integralism we mean talk of "regime change," integralism
as a present political project, then I disagree. It is both
impossible and, more importantly, simply wrong to found a
Catholic regime on something like a *coup d'état*. A Catholic
social order cannot be imposed by force on an unwilling
populace. If we want a Catholic social order, we had best
begin by converting our non-Catholic neighbor, although
it might be wiser to begin by converting ourselves first, for
in fact few American Catholics have any glimmer of what
the Church teaches about the shaping and reshaping of
our public life or the manner in which Catholic culture
differs from Protestant.

But there are other ideas. That of Catholic intentional
communities has roots in numerous nineteenth-century
Catholic colonization projects and never ceased to attract
Catholic attention. And rightly so, for so long as it is seen
as simply one tactic among many for how to deal with an
increasingly hostile or indifferent culture, it is a reasonable
idea. But such intentional communities must remember
our Lord's command to preach the Gospel to all nations.

Catholic intentional communities are simply a means, first to acquire a more or less secure base for ourselves and our families, to allow the faith to develop and flourish as a way of life, and then to try to go out to convert our neighbors. They must not be seen as akin to the Amish who seem content to live their own lives and leave everyone else alone.

In the early Church, Catholics lived almost always in danger of martyrdom, opposed by an openly hostile state. Their response was to live out the Gospel, and when the opportunity arose, to convert their neighbors and the entire culture. *That* must be our ultimate aim, however unlikely it appears of realization now. Anything else, any compromise with secular modernity, however expressed, is a betrayal both of our Lord's commandment and our own vocation.

THOMAS STORCK *is the host of the WCAT radio/TV program "The Open Door," a contributing editor of the* New Oxford Review, *and a member of the editorial board of* The Chesterton Review. *His latest book is* Economics: An Alternative Introduction *(XIII Books, 2024).*

Against Apocalyptic Whiggism

EDWIN DYGA

E ARE ASKED TO CONSIDER whether the "American experiment" is "exhausted." The answer largely depends on how this experiment is characterized, and a distant observer of American social and political trends, such as I, is perhaps not the best diagnostician. Nevertheless, setting aside the merits of the experiment itself, and assuming a polity has self-propagation as its core functional interest, it could be argued that America's exhaustion is proportional to the extent to which her citizens still retain some semblance of *civic vitality*. Judging by the willingness of many to engage in the bitterly litigated controversies of the present era (often at great risk not only to their professional standing and livelihood but their physical safety), it certainly appears that the collective American public does indeed retain this *will to live*.

Symposia such as this are a reminder that evidence of resistance is evidence of hope, and thus the promise of a better life. The problem is, therefore, how to channel this remaining vitality in an increasingly hostile environment. But before this can be properly addressed, what of the "experiment" itself?

Ernest Lee Tuveson's *Redeemer Nation: The Idea of America's Millennial Role* is an invaluable study of American political theology, its inherently utopian tendencies, and their inevitable dystopian consequences. Tuveson illustrates how a deformed Protestant reading of the Book of Revelation set the intellectual scene for our age of progressive ideology. By confusing the City of God with the City of Man, American Protestants saw redemption as attainable in the mundane world by vanquishing the enemies of God, which was to be a temporal, historical process. Secularized through the Enlightenment, this view has produced what Tuveson refers to as an "apocalyptic Whiggism" in American thought.[1] It can be detected in political agendas across the spectrum: from progressivism's projects of social re-engineering at home to *faux*-conservatism's messianic export of liberal democracy abroad. Both spring from the same source: a belief in the perfectibility of the individual and society. "The discovery of America," Tuveson writes, "and later the American Revolution, were placed in a sequence of victories beginning with the Reformation."[2]

If I read Tuveson correctly, he believes that the foundation of America was based on the presumed truth of this heretical proposition. America, of course, is not a "project" but a homeland — conceiving it otherwise risks fostering a universalistic agenda that recognizes no terrestrial borders. By identifying the Puritan spirit of democratic idealism as fundamental to the development of American national identity, Ralph Waldo Emerson similarly suggested that the "history of America is the history of the conquest of the world by Massachusetts."[3] Though American vitality has not yet been completely exhausted, the experiment to which its people have been subject may indeed have proven itself morally bankrupt. What Tuveson describes has pervaded all aspects of the public life. The process has deformed even the attitudes and worldview of those who ostensibly oppose it. Writing for *The New Criterion's* "Symposium on Democracy in America," Daniel J. Mahoney acknowledges that supporters of Donald Trump are "very

---

[1]   Ernest Lee Tuveson, *Redeemer Nation: The Idea of America's Millennial Role* (Chicago, IL: University of Chicago Press, 1968), p. 24.

[2]   Ibid.

[3]   This is an attributed statement that does not appear as a direct quotation from Emerson's published work; however, the general sentiment can be located, notably, in the collection of his "Miscellanies": J. E. Cabot (ed.), *The Works of Ralph Waldo Emerson* Vol. XI (Boston and New York: Fireside Edition, 1909 [1878]).

much a product of the social and moral dislocations that have transformed the country over the last half century." When elites become "addicted to ideological abstractions," he writes, civil institutions and the intellectual life become destabilized.[4]

American Catholics are fortunate because their faith has spared them despair at this grim situation. Present circumstances bring to mind the history of Zentrum, a German political party founded on the principles of Catholic social thought, which gained significant influence despite operating in a political environment that was not only explicitly Protestant but embraced an official *Kulturkampf* against the Church. In his *Historia Antykultury* ("The History of Anticulture"), the late Polish social commentator Krzysztof Karoń credits the success of this small party to the comprehensive worldview that a Catholic intellectual tradition could offer a state plagued by sectarianism, radical socialist agitation, and liberal upheaval. In the face of such turmoil, Zentrum presented "a social program which, while supported by Catholic Social Thought, was nevertheless a *rational program* capable of being accepted by adherents of other religions."[5]

This is not a strategy of withdrawal and retreat. The Apocalyptic Whiggism referred to earlier by Tuveson renders attempts at forming an archipelago of so-called Benedict Options a fool's errand. The effective erasure of borders we witness across the West does not affect national frontiers alone but also makes establishing autonomous Catholic communities impossible *within* the political sphere. No alternative to the secular progressive order—even if privately practiced—can be permitted to exist in the face of an ideology animated by a religious zeal and belief in its own eschatological righteousness. Withdrawal is just a

---

[4] Daniel J. Mahoney, "Tocqueville versus Progressive Democracy" *The New Criterion* Vol. 43, Issue 2 (Oct. 2024), p. 19.
[5] Krzysztof Karoń, *Historia Antykultury 1.0* (1st corr. ed.; Warsaw, Poland: Key4, 2019 [2018]), p. 357. The quote is the writer's translation, with emphasis added.

euphemism for retreat, and cowardice will only embolden the fanatical vindictiveness of those who hate the Church for the promise of civilizational renewal she offers.

Enlightenment-derived ideologies are messianic in their core character. In this sense, they are all heretical and bastardized versions of the Christianity to which they set themselves in opposition. Secular messianism is more vicious in its zeal because it is absent the Christian virtues. What Catholicism offers is an already existing program that simply needs to be applied to contemporary systems governance. The phenomenal ascent of Zentrum demonstrated a viable alternative based on *Rerum Novarum*, the encyclical of Leo XIII. With this legacy, it marginalized other dissenting movements on the liberal and extreme left.[6] There is no reason why a Catholic movement today should not be capable of replicating this success: the essential nature of the problems our civilization presently faces is comparable to that of pre-war Germany (in type if not in magnitude), and we possess the intellectual framework to address them. What is lacking is a kind of militancy that would allow a Catholic movement to withstand assaults against it — indeed, even to flourish in the inherently hostile climate of secular modernity.

What would be more effective than disappearing into the hills is a steady but uncompromising reassertion of the Catholic presence in the public square. To achieve this, a collective awareness of our *intentional* Catholic identity must be rekindled. But for this one key defect — caused mainly through the collapse of Church leadership — we find ourselves in a similar position to the late-nineteenth- and early twentieth-century Catholics of Protestant Germany. Society is starved for alternatives to the stale *status quo*, but one is available, if only it could be systematized into a form that can be rationally communicated to those most receptive to its message. Fortunately, contemporary Catholic advocates have already contributed to this task. To sight one

---

[6]   Ibid., pp. 355–356.

notable example, John Horvat II illustrates in his *Return to Order* how a Catholic worldview can be practically applied to a system of cultural as well as economic and political revival.[7] This is achieved through a rational exposition of normative policy proposals that could be acceptable to any social group irrespective of its own faith tradition.

The American Catholic who wishes to engage assertively in the public square must acknowledge that mainstream popular culture has become so distorted that his ethos will naturally appear *reactionary* in the eyes of the un- or misinformed. I would recommend that this fact be embraced, without fear or compunction. The alternative, which is far too often encountered, is for Catholics to harmonize with the world for the sake of maintaining a comity that has proven ultimately to be of no benefit to the health of the Church or her flock. In *The Church and the State* Thomas Molnar describes how the integration of Catholics into American life had the effect of limiting their imagination as to the "political and social forms" by which a nation could be governed.[8] The result was not only the continued paganization of the public square but the de-Catholicization of the Catholic citizen himself.[9] Needless to say, it is imperative that this imagination be rekindled. What civilization faces now is a future inspired by the worst aspects of the past: a neo-Babelist world ruled by the morality of the longhouse.[10] Being aware of this imports a sense of responsibility because we have an obligation to the communities in which we live. Molnar does not suggest that we politicize our religion, merely that we engage in the political life of the nation:

[7] John Horvat II, *Return to Order: From a Frenzied Economy to an Organic Society* (York, PA: York Press, 2013).

[8] Thomas Molnar, *The Church and the State: The Catholic Tradition as an Integral Element of Western Political Thought* (Providence, RI: Cluny, 2018 [1980]), p. 167.

[9] Ibid., p. 160.

[10] As to the latter, see: Jonathan Keeperman (a.k.a. Lom3z), "What is the Longhouse," *First Things* (online) <firstthings.com> (Feb. 16, 2023; accessed April 1, 2025).

The objective—internal restoration of the Church and resumption of its role as a moral guide of society—is so vital, spiritually so decisive, that it cannot be left to the bishops alone, and certainly not to the ecclesiastical bureaucracies. War is too important a matter, as the saying goes, to be left to the generals.[11]

America was a more confident and culturally robust nation when it could provide an Archbishop Fulton Sheen to the world. By corollary, the archbishop's own public service was arguably responsible for much of that nation's confidence and moral strength. The doctrines of Catholicism—rooted as they are in an objective truth discernible through Thomistic thought—are immovable. We have witnessed where apologetic compromises with a "pluralist state" lead. Molnar describes how such an order "can fast degenerate into a vehicle for a particular ideology," elevating its objectives "through privileged means, until it reaches a virtual monopoly position."[12] Invariably, this leads to the subordination of the Catholic worldview to its antithesis. The *intentional* Catholic would therefore benefit from the meditations of such uncompromising thinkers as Nicolás Gómez Dávila, whose aphorisms can be an effective antidote to the derailing temptations of secular modernity.[13] Little known in the Anglophone West, he stands out as an intellectual who did not use the "reactionary" label as a pejorative—and neither should we.

Thus, we return to the current state of the American experiment. While Tuveson identifies this root in Protestant millennialism, it should be noted that Catholicism too has often been criticized for its universalizing

---

[11] Molnar, *op. cit.*, pp. 173–174.

[12] Ibid., pp. 164–165.

[13] Nicolás Gómez Dávila, *The Authentic Reactionary: Selected Scholia of Nicolás Gómez Dávila*, Ramon Elani (trans.) (North Augusta, SC: Arcana Europa, 2023 [2020]). An earlier bilingual edition of his selected aphorisms was *Scholia to an Implicit Text* (Bogotá, Colombia: Villegas Editores, 2013).

tendency. However, the universal truth of Catholicism is best expressed in particular forms — one of which is through the unique cultural and historical experience of the American nation. American national identity — its genesis and nature — need not be rooted in heretical abstracts. The Protestant ideas on which America was founded implied the thing they protested against; one could say that Catholicism was therefore latent in America's identity from the beginning. A literary and cultural tradition that does not play into an Apocalyptic Whig framework has always been within reach. It is a tradition that recognizes the fallen state of mankind and seeks redemption before God but also recognizes our responsibility to the *res publica*. It is a tradition rooted in the particularities of place and people. Though it is often associated with the cultural heritage of a traditionally "WASP" Southern agrarian civilization, or the political legacies of paleoconservatism, it is not surprising that its revival is dominated by Catholic thinkers, converts, and men of letters.[14] These worlds and worldviews may seem vanquished by rapacious modernity, but what appears defeated is merely dormant, and thus ripe for rediscovery.

∞ ∞ ∞

EDWIN DYGA, *KHS, has a background in legal practice and government relations. He is the founder of the* Sydney Traditionalist Forum *and editor of the* Observer & Review. *He writes from Sydney, Australia.*

---

[14]   Edwin Dyga, "Prospects for Paleoconservatism" *Observer & Review* (2023) Vol. 1, Issue 1 (No. 1), *circa* pp. 33–34. As for the role of the Catholic novelist in democratic society, see: Trevor Cribben Merrill, *The Situation of the Catholic Novelist* Wiseblood Essays in Contemporary Culture (Milwaukee, WI: Wiseblood Books, 2021). My attention was recently also drawn to Gracjan Kraszewski's book *Catholic Confederates: Faith and Duty in the Civil War South* (Kent, OH: Kent State University Press, 2020), in which the author illustrates Catholicism's presence in a region dominated by Baptist, Methodist, Presbyterian, and other Protestant denominations. To suggest that Catholic tradition is foreign to the genesis of the American nation is nonsense.

21

The Kingship of Christ and the Catholic Counterworld

ROBERT MCTEIGUE, S.J.

Do not put your trust in princes, in mortals, in whom there is no help (Psalm 146:3)

THAT'S MY STARTING POINT FOR politics. When I first began to write this, another American presidential election was looming. American Catholics, historically, have been desperate to prove that they're really *real* Americans. Reassurances about American Catholics not having divided loyalties are repeated. (Those reassurances, practically speaking, have become more and more convincing in the past sixty-five years.)

Papal warnings regarding the heresy of Americanism are little known. I didn't even hear about them until post-graduate studies, and I was assured not to worry about them, because "Americanism wasn't a real heresy — and Leo XIII proves that European prelates [of a certain vintage] just didn't understand what America was all about." I was never encouraged to read what Pope Leo actually wrote about the matter. I finally did read his encyclicals *Longinquina oceani* and *Testem benevolentiae nostrae,* and now I suspect that my professors might not have given me the best guidance after all.

The awkward silences and possible misdirections begin to multiply and intensify by the time we get to Pius XI and his establishment of the Solemnity of Christ the King via *Quas primas.* This solemnity and its accompanying documentation could have caused continuing embarrassment for Catholics in America who wanted to be welcomed as authentic, really *real* Americans. The solemnity is very much based on, well, the *Kingship* of Christ, His rights as King, the universality of His sovereignty, and even the hierarchical and teleological nature of creation. Language like that doesn't get you invited to the better parties, and it certainly doesn't put government coins in diocesan or institutional coffers.

Consider this summary of the Kingship of Christ:

> From the birth of the Catholic Church on Calvary and the solemn promulgation of her mission on Pentecost, the Kingdom of God in its essence has been present in the world.... The Kingdom of God or the rule of Christ the King is present in its integrity only in so far as the whole social life of states, political and economic, is permeated with the influence of the Church. To put it in other terms, Christ fully reigns only when the Program for which he died is accepted as the one true way to peace and order in the world, and social structures in harmony with it are evolved.[1]

It's no wonder that Catholic Al Smith's presidential campaign failed. Senator John F. Kennedy didn't want to carry the Catholic "baggage" draped about Smith's neck, so he met with Protestant ministers in Houston in September 1960, declaring that his Catholic faith and practice could be safely compartmentalized for the greater good. Kennedy proved that Catholic identity need not be an impediment to American political success.

Twenty-three years later, almost to the day, self-identified Catholic governor of New York Mario Cuomo addressed Notre Dame University, providing concepts and vocabulary to many Catholics seeking political success in America. These politicians could be "personally opposed to abortion, but..." and would never dream of "imposing" their morality on others.

---

[1] Fr. Denis Fahey C.S.Sp., *The Kingship of Christ and Organized Naturalism* (1943), pp. 32–33.

Almost forty years later, in a "statement of principles," sixty self-identified Catholic members of Congress claimed that their Catholic faith influences their congressional actions and that denial of Holy Communion for their support for legal abortion would be "contradictory." So much for being "personally opposed" to abortion!

What happened between 1960 and 2021 that resulted in public commitments and demands that would have been unintelligible to Kennedy and unthinkable to Cuomo? That's a long and complicated story. Yet we can point to one change that facilitated the shift in stance from Kennedy and Cuomo to current congressmen.

In *Quas primas*, Pius XI declared:

> The last Sunday of October seemed the most con-venient of all for this purpose, because it is at the end of the liturgical year, and thus the feast of the Kingship of Christ sets the crowning glory upon the mysteries of the life of Christ already commemorated during the year, and, before cele-brating the triumph of all the Saints, we proclaim and extol the glory of him who triumphs in all the Saints and in all the Elect. Make it your duty and your task, Venerable Brethren, to see that sermons are preached to the people in every parish to teach them the meaning and the importance of this feast, that they may so order their lives as to be worthy of faithful and obedient subjects of the Divine King.[2]

The Kingship of Christ, celebrated toward the end of the liturgical year, as its crown, is also acknowledged in *all of the saints and feasts of the preceding year*. The reign of Christ is acknowledged from the Church's beginning and in the consummation of creation at the eschaton.

Forty years after *Quas primas*, the solemnity is put at the very end of the liturgical year, *after* the celebration of All Saints. The Kingship of Christ, consequently, can be

---

[2] Pope Pius XI, *Quas primas* (1925), §20.

viewed as exclusively eschatological — His reign begins as
time ends. On this view, after the Ascension, the King is
an absentee landlord who will collect the rent at the end
of time. Until then, we're on our own, and Christ has not
much to say about how we live. Is this an oversimplifica-
tion? Almost certainly. But that does not mean it is untrue.

Since at least the time of the French Revolution, the
temptation has been to banish or at least reduce to irrele-
vancy the claims of Christ, making them less intrusive, less
commanding, less forbidding, and, finally, nonjudgmental.
This is what the uncrowned Christ looks like.

What's the moral of this story for Catholics in America today? How about this: "The time has not come for
Jesus Christ to reign? Well, then the time has not come
for governments to last."[3]

As I write this, the second Trump administration is a
few months old. Dire warnings of "Christian nationalism"
abound. Indeed, we're reminded by those who are sure
they know all too well about such things that "Christian
nationalism" is the polite face of the darker, even more
menacing demon of "white supremacy."

In certain neighborhoods of social media, the phrase
"Christ Is King" is taken as a rallying cry. In other neighborhoods of social media, "Christ Is King" is the opening
act in a new wave of antisemitism, which will fully reveal
itself soon. Very soon. Any moment now. Just you wait....
Meanwhile, the group Catholics for Catholics works toward
"inspiring a new wave of Catholicism and patriotism in
America," sponsoring a Catholic Prayer for America Gala
at Trump's residence at Mar-a-Lago. Many clerics of various ranks and a wide array of canonical statuses attended.
There was eucharistic adoration. Could this be taken as a
sign of impending . . . what . . . exactly?

Prominent Protestant scholars and pastors discourse
about the prospect of various American states returning

---

[3] Louis-Édouard-François-Desiré Cardinal Pie, bishop of Poitiers,
France, to Emperor Napoleon III (1856).

to the *status quo ante* — states with established churches (and perhaps *only* established churches), with both law and pastoring understood to be forms of ministry supported by the state. Some even talk (albeit guardedly) about the emergence (someday) of a "Christian prince."

Protestants have much more experience with managing confessional states in America than Catholics do. Connecticut, Massachusetts, South Carolina, Virginia, North Carolina, Georgia, and Delaware all had established churches. The state of Maryland is a special case. Founded in 1632 by Cecil Calvert, Lord Baltimore, an English Catholic nobleman, the state sheltered persecuted English Catholics. The Act of Toleration of 1649 gave legal protections and freedom of worship to both Catholics and Protestants in Maryland — and no one else. Never could Maryland be described as a true confessional state with Catholicism as the established church. Following the Glorious Revolution of 1688 in England, the Act of Toleration in Maryland was revoked, with Catholics disenfranchised and persecuted. In sum, Catholics in America have no experience of managing an established church in a confessional state.

Almost no Catholic in America today has even heard of, much less read and understood, encyclicals such as *Mirari vos, Qui pluribus, In supremae dignitatis, Non abbiamo bisogno,* or *Divini Redemptoris.* Consequently, I think it's safe to say that there will not be a popular groundswell calling for the anointing of anyone as a neo-Hapsburg governor of any of America's fifty states. Indeed, given that precious few Catholics in America today have even heard of Fr. John Courtney Murray, S.J., I believe that most American Catholics couldn't begin to have an intelligent conversation about any aspect of Church-state relations.

So, why all the fuss? Admittedly, I have been somewhat sardonic in my account of the last few months in American politics. I did so to prove a point: *Almost nothing significant in Church-state relations will change in America in the next generation.* I say this because the roots of secularism are so deeply embedded in our current culture. In addition, the sin of "religious indifferentism" (wittingly or unwittingly) masquerading as "tolerance" is deeply embedded in the lives of American Christians, just as several popes had warned. Moreover, the roots of Enlightenment deism, rationalism, and naturalism are embedded further still. No established church, no confessional state, will appear in any American state as long as Americans swear allegiance to the Constitution as it was written. Please note that I do not say this as a boast, a lament, or a warning, but simply as a statement of fact.

I think Catholics in America need to overcome their ignorance of Catholic political thought and Church history. They also need to drink deeply from the precious spring of realism. Next, they need to shout Psalm 146:3 repeatedly. Then they need to get to work.

What could that work possibly look like? Candidly, Catholics in America are more likely to get a better "deal" with a Trump administration than they ever would have with a Harris administration. Likewise, they would get a better deal with a Vance administration than a Newsom administration. Consequently, Catholics should act accordingly. Catholic individuals and institutions would do well to wean themselves off Caesar's coin. They must reorient themselves so as not to outsource the corporal works of mercy to the state. They must forswear even the appearance of having become NGOs, however well-intentioned they may be. That process of weaning and forswearing should keep us all busy for a good long time.

Consider this: "The Church's function is not to adapt Christianity to the world, nor even to adapt the world to Christianity; her function is to maintain a counterworld within the world."[4] This is what I would like to see: Catholics in America maintaining a counterworld. In that counterworld, Catholics would prioritize worthy worship.

---

[4] Gómez Dávila, *op. cit.*

History shows that when man, in justice and charity, gives God His due via worship, man is more likely to love and serve his neighbor, spiritually and temporally, for the love of God. In the Catholic counterworld, formation of families and places of learning and the arts would flourish. Such communities would offer a viable and attractive alternative to the secularism that the Reformation and the Enlightenment helped to engender. Perhaps, on a long enough timeline, asymptotically, polities in America would recognize that "Christ Is King" is more than just a mantra or a rallying cry. Instead, it would be seen as a perpetual truth that has been slowly incarnated in various times and places, in differing degrees, even in America. Perhaps then our children will sing Revelation 4:10–11: "The twenty-four elders fall down before him who sits on the throne and worship him who lives for ever and ever. They lay their crowns before the throne and say: 'You are worthy, our Lord and God, to receive glory and honor and power, for you created all things, and by your will they were created and have their being.'"

∞ ∞ ∞

Fr. Robert McTeigue, s.j., *is a member of the U.S. Eastern Province of the Society of Jesus. He is the host of* The Catholic Current, *a radio talk show that airs on* The Station of the Cross Catholic Media Network, *and is a member of the National Ethics Committee of the Catholic Medical Association. His latest books from Ignatius Press are* Real Philosophy for Real People: Tools for Truthful Living *(2020) and* Christendom Lost and Found: Meditations for a Post Post-Christian Era *(2022). Fr. McTeigue's work can be found at heraldofthegospel.org.*

22

The Strange Soul of
Our Secularist Empire

JASON M. MORGAN

N AMERICA, POLITICS IS PROTES-
tantism, and Protestantism is politics. American
politics is textual, explicit, quasi-metaphysical,
performative, obsessive, and deeply conflicted. American
politicians mix biblical references with Lockean clap-
trap as naturally as they invoke God's blessing prior to
launching cruise missiles into a foreign city. Freedom is
the American political mantra, and Joshua, destroyer of
metropoles, is American politicians' ideal. What violence
men do on Earth is sanctioned in Heaven, the violence
being the act that both confesses and confirms the power
of the biblical God at work in the affairs of nations. The
Pilgrims pogromed the Indians and gave glory to Yahweh,
then repented only because they had been insufficiently
zealous in exterminating the enemies of the Protestant
faith from the Protestants' new world. There were still,
behold, Catholics to drive out of the Arizona deserts and
Texas hill country. And so it was done. Even today the
Pilgrims' progeny call on God and George Washington,
on Moses and Abraham Lincoln, on Elijah and Thomas
Jefferson as they prepare to further expand the boundar-
ies of God's secular reign. Presidents get prayed over by
Baptists. Even the Catholic Joe Biden had to act like a
Protestant conqueror to win the Oval Office. Politics and
Protestantism: together they form the national character,
the strange, topsy-turvy soul of a secularist empire at once
obsessed with religious revival, democratizing foreigners,
and intermittently carpet-bombing them.

The Protestants who rewrote American place names thought they had left Europe behind them, but everywhere they went they saw the ghosts of the Roman Church they had tried dismantling. Americans' centuries-old distrust of Catholics as somehow a Vatican fifth-column springs from their sense of being a uniquely chosen people, sifted out of history. But this sense of chosenness is surely an attempt to salve the conscience that knows, somehow, that rebellion against God is not a mark of holiness but of damnation. That the "founding fathers" of the American heresy hated papists almost as much as they hated kings is not merely coincidentally connected to Milton's celebration of Satan as political hero. Exiled from grace, Protestants forever seek a second-best salvation in politics. Hence, the hordes of WASPs clearing out continents and oceans in deliverance of the gospel of the repeater rifle, the ballot box, and the neutron bomb. Make way for the Presbyterians, the Methodists, the Unitarians even, for God has given them a new commandment: Save the world and incinerate the parts of it that do not cooperate with this plan of salvation. Only Catholics stand in the way of the completion of the Reformation, which one glimpsed at Hiroshima and Nagasaki and may again glimpse soon in Tehran. John F. Kennedy denied the Protestants their Armageddon in Cuba. The Protestant curia in Washington, that cabal of permanent revolutionaries whose name now is "Deep State" but whose members are always legion, cleared Kennedy away so that war, holy war, could continue forever. Rome may be the Eternal City, but Washington is the New Jerusalem, and with that the Old World religion cannot compete.

Catholics once resisted, it is true. Not everyone, of course. Irony of ironies, "Maryland" is handmaiden to Caesar the same as is "New Hampshire." But somewhere along the way, Catholics, who for a long while made, on the whole, a manly show of defiance of the Protestants' politico-evangelical fever dances, gave in to the spiritual currents of the land. Liberation theology? Sorry, Latin

Americans, that's a New England vintage. The longer Catholics sojourned in America, the more Protestantism seeped into the faith. Rome held out against the American fusion of sermons and stump speeches, even though Rome didn't fully understand it. By the time Rome caught on to what was happening to American Catholicism, though, it was too late. Concerned theologians, including some popes, saw the corrosive effect on society when religion and government are *separated* and called it "Americanism." But nearly everything in American religious history suggests that religion and politics are the same thing. Catholics eventually came to believe that, too. The separation of church and state? Arlington Cemetery is arrayed with crosses, stars, and crescents. Name one person buried there who was martyred for a faith other than the American creed. "In God We Trust" is still our national motto. It's printed right there on the money the Federal Reserve counterfeits, the money created out of thin air to fund wars and abortions. Alas, I once attended a Catholic Mass deep in the heart of Alabama at which the congregation and the priest sang, as worship music, that call to soak the field in enemy blood, "The Battle Hymn of the Republic." If there is a flag in Heaven, it is surely Old Glory, to which even God must stand and salute. There is no separation of church and state in America. There is only America, crowned by the Almighty (or so the Americans would have it — God may see things differently). Catholics could once make the distinction between faith and fallen politics, but now the takeover is almost complete. And it's spreading.

The fact is that Rome, too, fell before the Americanization of the world. Catholicism as we know it now is essentially Pilgrimism dressed in the fripperies of deracinated natural law. The Americanist fingerprints of John Courtney Murray, S.J., are all over the documents of the Second Vatican Council, for example, including his baby, *Dignitatis humanae*. All roads lead to Rome became all religions lead to Heaven. God bless America, where faith gets you only so far because to be saved you have to testify. (Testifying with machine guns in Afghan villages is even better than making altar calls at your local evangelical church/coffee-shop.) It was the Americans who broke Catholicism and remodeled it on the Declaration of Independence. But you can hardly blame one Jesuit, then or now — the late Jorge Bergoglio having out-Murrayed the original — for the dismantling of the Roman religion. Not even Rome could resist the U.S. of A. Protestantism boomeranged clear across the Atlantic Ocean, spun for a season of frenzy over North America, crept into the Catholic seminaries and immigrant strongholds there, and then swung back across the ocean to Rome. Americanism is the heresy of church-state separation and also the reality of church and state indistinguishably combined. American exceptionalism is just as invincible, it would seem, as American Catho-lics have always known it to be. Not even Rome stands a chance against it. When the next pope dresses in jeans and a t-shirt and sports a stars-and-stripes tattoo, then you will know that the transformation of Catholicism into Americanism is done. For now we'll have to settle for a pontiff in a White Sox cap. But we're getting there.

And so here we are some two and a half centuries since a rogues' gallery of slaveholding deists and assorted Enlightenment revolutionaries scrawled some lines on parchment in a colonial backwater and set in motion a cataclysm in continental Christianity. We are all democrats, all deciders in the religion-state the founders bequeathed to us. American Catholics had little choice but to low with the herd. Freedom! Democracy! Or death! (Or all three!) The priesthood of all believers preaches, in some corners, the genital mutilation of minors, and in others the "New American Century." Children are dismembered in our Christian America, and the best the Catholics sitting on the Supreme Court can do about it is to remand the question to the states, where the notion of infanticide is proving, on the whole, very popular with voters. America

is truly exceptional in that religion has no braking power
on the evils of government. Quite the opposite. Catholicism in America — which is to say, more often than not,
Americanism in a Roman collar — is powerless to stop the
machinery of progress from grinding up those in the way,
whether they're the fentanyl corpses littering Appalachia,
the tranq zombies swaying in the streets of Philadelphia,
or the poor and the trafficked in virtually every corner of
the nation. Washington, D.C., and its suburbs, meanwhile,
are enjoying a building boom. War in Ukraine and Gaza is
big business. War with Iran and China will be even bigger.
Catholics will be right there on the front lines killing for
democracy alongside their American brothers (and sisters!).
For God has blessed America, and will continue to do so
only so long as we provide sufficient human sacrifice. I'm
told that Catholic chaplains have had a hard time in the
military these past two decades. Are there any Catholics
left in uniform, though? The last holdouts seem to have
left the service rather than pump themselves full of vac-
cines made from aborted children (contrary to the advice
of the Holy Pfizer, I mean Father). To be a Catholic in
American political life is to be a Protestant, or to be, as
John Kennedy learned the hard way, wholly superfluous.

But still hope springs eternal. There emerges in the
twilight of our republic a group of people who say that
only Catholicism can save America. I marvel at those who
seem not to have noticed that Catholicism *is* America now.
Because America is Catholicism, which is to say, Protestantism. The resistance is a mirage, for the Christians in the
West have long since gone over to the side of Melanchthon
and Calvin. The Spirit of 1776 conquered the Roman
religion decades ago. A contingent of American Catholics
looks to the Vatican to cure what ails America. It is a
hair-of-the-dog gambit, at best, but not a cure. American
Catholics who call on Rome for succor will be surprised,
or maybe not, to find that Rome will deploy to America
priests who are even more American than the American

Catholics are. Pilgrims did not civilize the wilderness. The wilderness swallowed up Christendom, and now we are out of luck. There may be, far beyond the horizon, a spiritual renewal prepared for the land of our birth. But if so, it will not be named after an Italian mapmaker. It will instead have a connection to a Roman metropolis that has also shed its unfortunate association with the world's only remaining Protestant theocracy. But all that is the work of ages hence. For the far foreseeable future, American Catholicism, like America itself, and like Protestantism, is a dead letter, a failed project, an experiment hateful to the living God.

∞ ∞ ∞

JASON M. MORGAN *teaches history, philosophy, and international relations at Reitaku University in Kashiwa, Japan. He is a contributing editor of the* New Oxford Review *and the author of* Law and Society in Imperial Japan: Suehiro Izutarō and the Search for Equity *(Cambria Press) and, with J. Mark Ramseyer,* The Comfort Women Hoax: A Fake Memoir, North Korean Spies, and Hit Squads in the Academic Swamp *(Encounter Books).*

23

America Possessed:
The Demon of Counterfeit Reality

THADDEUS KOZINSKI

T IS WELL KNOWN THAT PEOPLE IN a psychotic state of fear will believe anything, no matter how absurd and destructive, as long as it promises them a way out of the torturing fear. Every would-be totalitarian knows this, and that is why totalitarianism is most effectively ushered in by a mass-trauma event followed by an arbitrary assignment of blame, a scapegoating campaign, and then a recipe for fear mitigation. If you follow "reality" by first believing *this* horror story (now you have an object for the free-floating anxiety), scapegoating *these* people (now you belong to the community of the righteous), and following *these* mandates (now you have the path to salvation as well as the antidote to the horror), your loneliness, fear, and guilt will cease. But I think there is a deeper explanation for the transformation of so many postmodern relativists into ritual scapegoaters in March 2020.

Human beings are inevitably ordered to the transcendent, the good, the true, and the beautiful, and we are ordered to these not as separate individuals but by and in community. We crave to know, love, and celebrate reality, to live within it and for it, even to give our lives to and for it, but we want most of all to do these things *with others*. We want the good for ourselves, of course, but we cannot have it all for ourselves. We must want it for and with others, for the good cannot be enjoyed alone. Reality is a common good, one that increases and deepens the more people know, love, and share it. What we want most of all is for our political community to express, authorize, and

be founded upon reality, for we know intuitively that if
it is founded upon mere human will, however apparently
benevolent or democratic, it will tyrannize us. Aristotle
expresses this Platonic insight:

> When the community made up of several villages
> is complete it is then a city, possessing the limit
> of every self-sufficiency, practically speaking, and
> though it originates for the sake of life it exists for
> the sake of the good life. Consequently, every city is
> by nature, if, that is, the first communities also are.
> For the city is the end of those communities and
> nature is an end, since we say that a thing's nature
> is the sort of thing it is when its generation has
> been completed (as in the case of a human being,
> a horse, or a house). Further, that for the sake of
> which something is, or its end, is best and self-
> sufficiency is both an end and best.... By nature,
> then, the drive towards such a community exists
> in everyone; but the first to set one up is respon-
> sible for very great goods. For as human beings
> are the best of all animals when perfected, so they
> are the worst when divorced from law and right.[1]

"Right" and "law" are common goods that cannot be
adequately established through or fully possessed by individuals or families. These perfecting goods are found only
in the larger and more complex polis, and, as Aristotle
says, a man who does not live in a polis, or does not need
to, is either a beast or a god. But, according to liberalism,
right and law are not and could never be based upon the
good, upon reality, for being mere contractual edicts they
express nothing more than human will. And this is as
it should be. Liberalism's privatization of the good not
only "divorces us from law and right," thus making us the
"worst of animals," but also makes us crave and attempt to
establish reality-based law and good-expressing right. We

---

[1] *The Politics of Aristotle*, Translated by Peter Simpson (Chapel Hill,
NC: University of North Carolina Press, 1997), Bk. I, 2; pp. 29-33.

cannot help it, for nature cannot be eradicated. It can be repressed, however, and when it is, what ensues is a monster.

In the absence of a coordinated psychological operation of terror, torture, and scapegoating, citizens of liberal regimes tend to fixate on their free-floating anxiety, assuage their loneliness, and satisfy their inexorable desire for a communally shared reality and an authoritative good by joining together in worship (sometimes authentic religious worship, but also the cults of career, sport, moneymaking, shopping, etc.). For the saintly among us who, being god-like, do not need the crude laws of the polis as much as others, they are perfected well enough by the reality they know personally and mystically through Divine Revelation and the Tao, that is, without requiring the political publicization of the good; their anxiety, loneliness, and guilt are purged by their intimate relationship with God. But the vast majority of us need the polis as well as the Church, for they unite us, not in an isolated and isolating individualistic pursuit of happiness, but in the communal enjoyment of happiness, in the knowledge, love, and celebration of the good in the real.

The Catholic Church is a polis, indeed, the best one, and the perfect model for all other polises. But there is nature as well as grace, reason as well as faith, the temporal as well as the spiritual, and we are political animals as much as religious ones, citizens of the City of Man and, by grace, the City of God. God forbid that the Church would ever become a servant of the City of Man! Well, God did not forbid this. An official Vatican conference held in May 2021 supported the injection of the global population with an experimental serum. Not to mention the Vatican-mandated closing of churches, with priests refusing to hear confessions or give Last Rites, parishes all over the world mandating masks and "social distancing," and even using parishes as injection sites. Here we have the very custodians and mediators of ultimate reality, the pope and all the bishops of the Catholic Church, renouncing their sacred vocation to truth, embracing a counterfeit reality, and imposing it on the Catholics they are supposed to serve.

The totalitarianism to which we were subjected beginning in 2020 is best explained as the return of the repressed, and, as we know from horror movies, the form this return takes is always a monster. Observing the totalitarian monster birthed from the ontological and spiritual vacuum of liberalism rampaging around the globe claiming to be reality incarnate, and the billions following the monster blindly as he approached the cliff, we can see just how powerful our need is for institutions and authorities to be based upon reality. When Christ is dethroned, Antichrist is waiting in the wings, but we would rather have him than nothing. Global insanity was unleashed due to this primordial spiritual need having been repressed for so long and so extensively, giving birth to an existential fear grown to pathological levels, satiated and exacerbated by a counterfeit reality promulgated by a counterfeit authority offering a counterfeit savior from a counterfeit evil. In short, this is perhaps *the* demonstrative proof that Plato was right, though he did not know that the good would eventually come down from Heaven and live in a backwater town somewhere east of Athens.

The evil that entrenched itself at the heart of political and cultural power in America in 2020 not only purported to have authority over us but also, it seems, actually possessed it. For we gave it that authority. It is as if it had a *right* to be there. Exorcists tell us that exorcism only works when it can reveal the "legal" right a demon has somehow obtained to possess its victim, for only then can it undo this "contract," whether created by the curse of another or by the voluntary invitation of the victim. Nothing short of the undoing of that right can vanquish it. To accomplish this, the victim must renounce his idolatry—for all sin is a form of idolatry, putting something in the place of God—and then worship, explicitly and intentionally, Jesus Christ. The demon will leave only when the victim both renounces Satan *and* surrenders to Christ. The soul cannot remain neutral.

The demon that possesses America's ruling elite — and
let us not be so stupid as to think that Trump, Musk, and
friends are not also possessed by this demon — and through
them the collective soul, as it were, of our nation and the
West as a whole, has a right to be there as a result of both
a curse and a voluntary invitation. America was cursed
long ago, and it continues to be, by Freemasons and other
principled rejectors of Jesus Christ. But we Christians also
invited the demon in. We will never be able to exorcise
this demon by attempting to replace it with "medical freedom," "individual sovereignty," or "the will of the people."
These are counterfeit replacements for a freedom based
on the truth about the human person, created with an
immortal soul and teleologically ordered to the natural and
supernatural good, the sovereignty of the family, and all
other natural communities that organically and corporately
embody the common good, the will of God, and the divine
authority of the Church. Now, I am a proponent of the
natural, God-given freedoms and rights that legitimately
authorize the use of political, coercive power to secure
and protect them. But these freedoms and rights, properly understood as grounded in natural and supernatural
reality and interpreted definitively and authoritatively *only*
by the Catholic Church, are not necessarily the same as
the "American freedoms" granted to us, ostensibly, by the
Declaration of Independence and the U.S. Constitution.

Though rhetorically our rights come from "Nature and
Nature's God," there is, according to American political theology, no actual, historical religious tradition or institution
to give determinate meaning and theological authority to
such a claim, only unreal, ahistorical, abstract counterfeits
of the traditions of the Catholic Church, which *is* this religious tradition and institution, but can never be officially
recognized as such. As D.C. Schindler has demonstrated,
the "god" of the Declaration is not the Christian one but
an Enlightenment, deist, rationalist counterfeit. Thus, it has
only as much authority as it has rhetorical and moral power.

It was quite easy for later generations of rulers to completely ignore and even reject this artificial civil theology when it was no longer persuasive, and to replace it with progressivism, secularism, and now wokeism. That is because there was no universally or publicly recognized moral and spiritual authority in the American founding, just sundry Protestant opinions, the Constitution, and "We the People" (which means, in practice, the will of those empowered to represent the people). In short, American political power, both domestically and abroad, is authorized by nothing but itself. Inevitably it will employ its power under the conditions of modernity, meaning in a godless and self-referential manner. This is the main problem with the Catholic integralism of the Adrian Vermeule and Gladden Pappin variety. It is essentially Catholic Hobbesianism, with the true spiritual authority of the Church desacralized and profaned, nothing but blunt instrument for the will to power of "Catholics."

It is not that we have been gradually losing our rights, freedoms, and political power since, say, the Civil War; it is that we never really had them to begin with, for they were never grounded in real political authority. Real political authority is nothing but a participation in the transcendent spiritual reality and authority of God as mediated by His Church. The ultimate authority of God was revealed to us in its most pure form when it was utterly powerless: in Christ crucified. As the Church enters into her Passion in imitation of her Savior, we must be prepared to stay and suffer with her as she is crucified by the powers and principalities of the world. We must recognize and submit to true authority precisely when it is utterly powerless, as Mary and John did, and unmask and reject counterfeit authority when it is, seemingly, all-powerful, as it is now.

∞ ∞ ∞

THADDEUS KOZINSKI *is a teacher and writer. He is the author of four books, including* Modernity as Apocalypse: Sacred Nihilism and the Counterfeits of Logos *(Angelico Press) and writes at childrenbewareofidols.substack.com.*

Casting Down the Mighty, Lifting Up the Lowly

JOHN C. MÉDAILLE

S THE AMERICAN EXPERIMENT AN exhausted project? Questions of this kind are usually addressed at the level of either politics or culture, or maybe both. But one factor is usually missing: economics. Andrew Breitbart said that "politics is downstream of culture." True enough, but he should have added, " . . . and culture is downstream of breakfast." For a man must have breakfast before he accomplishes anything, and he must continue to eat each day if he is to continue his accomplishments. In truth, you cannot divorce culture from agriculture, or the industrial state from industrialism. The way we earn our daily bread conditions the way we think about ourselves and the world. And it conditions our politics.

The modern world in general, and Americans in particular, think in terms of capitalism, and a predatory capitalism at that. This system cannot survive in its present form. It is a philosophy and a practice of pure consumption for consumption's sake, with no higher purpose than increasing profits. But the proper *telos* of a proper economy is the material support of families and communities. That *telos* plays no role in our political or economic thinking. We don't even measure it, and hence we cannot say, with any degree of confidence, how well it is working. The *only* valid way to measure the success of an economy is to measure the strength of families and communities, which are precisely the things that are collapsing, even as our GDP increases.

A consumerist culture always ends up consuming itself. First it consumes its individuals, then its families, then its communities, then its natural resources, and finally, when there is nothing left to consume, it eats itself. We seem to be in this last stage: families are declining, communities deteriorating, and natural resources disappearing. The last thing to go will be the system itself, and that, most likely, in an orgy of violence.

We have heard, since the Reagan administration at least, that "government is not the solution; government is the problem." Despite this "small government" rhetoric, capitalism has *never* been able to distribute enough purchasing power to clear its own markets, and it has always relied on the government as the consumer of last resort. Indeed, the government never grew so fast as it did when the Liberal Party (we would say "Libertarian Party") came to power in England in 1832 or when the Republican "libertarians" triumphed after the Civil War and gave us the age of the Robber Barons. In that glorious age, the business cycle averaged less than four years, boom to bust, while public euphoria alternated with social depression in the same rapid succession.

That age would last until the Great Depression. Franklin D. Roosevelt's New Deal went some way toward redressing the balance between rich and poor. Of course, he was accused of being a "socialist" or worse, but in fact he saved capitalism for the capitalists. And he was served by a number of Catholics, such as Msgr. John Ryan (who was called "The Rt. Rev. New Dealer" by his opponents), who were well versed in Catholic social teaching. FDR regarded Pope Pius XI's 1931 encyclical *Quadragessimo anno* as "one of the greatest documents of the modern world." The New Deal would survive until the 1980s, when Reagan proclaimed its death with the slogan "Morning in America." But Reagan, despite his rhetoric, followed the pattern, expanding government and tripling the national debt. The difference was that he did so for the benefit of a single class. Rather than morning, the dark night of the Robber Barons returned, and it seems to have culminated in Donald Trump, with his cabinet of billionaires and talk-show hosts.

Those of us who grew up with the New Deal and now work in education know firsthand that our expectations were very different from those of our students. As a young graduate with a liberal-arts degree (paid for with the help of the G.I. Bill), I could command a salary sufficient to start a family, buy a home and a car, and do so without putting my wife to work. This is not the expectation of my students, nearly all whom, both men and women, are training for a career, knowing that one salary will not support a family. Add to that the fact that they are starting life with crushing debts from their education.

Can Catholics expect a place at the table of American politics? The better question would be: Do we have anything to *bring* to the table? There is no lack of Catholics in politics; there is a notorious lack of Catholic political thought in general, and Catholic social teaching in particular. This problem was brought to the fore recently when Vice President J.D. Vance, a Catholic no less, made the astounding connection between the *ordo amoris* and his administration's policy of "America First," between a practical principle (first aid those nearest to you) and a rivalrous nationalism. That he would use St. Augustine to support such nationalism is astounding enough, but nationalism is just a fancy word for tribalism. It is merely tribalism with better weapons and larger armies. Nationalism, beginning with tribalism, is the cause of every single war. Every. Single. One. Yes, even the Crusades. There are no exceptions. And this includes the two major wars that are occurring right now. Both are fought under the banners of "(Russia/ Ukraine/Israel/Palestine) First." Neither can end well.

I suspect Vance is the victim of an over concentration on Scholastic rationalism, something that frequently happens to Catholic converts and pious traditionalists. Such rationalism can be a useful tool, but never the final end, of theology. Taken as the end, it quickly becomes rationalism, and just as quickly it discovers that anything can be rationalized. Even nationalism. Even capitalism. But what it will never rationalize is lifting up the poor and casting down the mighty. American Catholics' "contribution" seems to be limited to denouncing abortion. Aside from that, we seem to be mainly on the side of those who are defending Dives and defunding Lazarus, even to the point of citing the *ordo amoris* to rationalize this failure of love. We have to do better than that.

So, what should we be doing? Some seek the answer in integralism, basically a fancy word for a theocracy, either in a strong or a weak form. But we have over a thousand years' experience with this system, and the results are not encouraging. It involved the Church in the dynastic struggles and the petty politics of rather petty princes. And the costs were ruinous, leading to the monetization of salvation through the sale of indulgences, the proximate cause of the Protestant Reformation. And the Reformers themselves quickly adopted this same integralism, uniting themselves with kings and princes or even, as in Geneva, with democracies. The plain fact of the matter is that bishops, cardinals, and popes are no less subject to the *libido dominandi*, the "lust for power," than is any king, prince, president, or banker. Indeed, the popes could be better tyrants than Henry VIII, better capitalists than Andrew Carnegie, better bankers than Andrew Mellon, better warmongers than Julius Caesar.

Further, it turns out that princes can play the integralist game as well as popes, demanding the right to hold the "two swords" of power and religion (using Pope Boniface VIII's rather tendentious interpretation of the "two swords" in the Gospel of Luke) and the right to control appointments and revenues, and even which papal documents could be promulgated within their lands. Indeed, the principle of "the separation of church and state" was first invoked to protect the Church *from* the state, which is why both the Stuart and Bourbon kings had Jesuit tracts on the separation of powers publicly burned by their public executioners.

The rich capitalists are more than happy to co-opt the Church and even become her biggest benefactors, lavishly supporting the Church, but only so long as she does not question their position or the source of their funds. Integralism doesn't threaten capitalists in the least, and they are the ones who most need to be threatened, to be cast down from their gold-plated toilets—err—thrones.

No, the answer does not lie in seizing power but in renouncing it. This is the answer found in Pope Gelasius's 494 letter to the Byzantine emperor, in which he said, "For there are two means, O emperor Augustus, by which the world is principally ruled: the sacred authority of pontiffs and the royal power." To translate Gelasius into modern jargon, the Church must "speak truth to power," and the truth she speaks is the truth of the Gospels, particularly the Gospel as it was expressed by Mary in her Magnificat, as the casting down of the mighty from their thrones and lifting up of the lowly. That is not a message the mighty like to hear. But we should shout it all the more. For while there must be a separation of the Church from political power, there can be no separation of the Church from politics. Indeed, the separation of power leaves the Church free to preach the Gospel and rebuke the princes. On occasion, every pulpit needs to be a soapbox, and the people in the pews need to hear from their pastors, especially on any subject that affects the "lifting up of the lowly."

The True Church, the *ekklesia* (a term from Greek politics meaning the assembly of the people), is protected by the institutional Church (or should be); the two are united but not identical.

We have an example of this in Pope Francis's rebuke of Vance, in which he refused to endorse the nationalism of "America First," or to banish the poor to some remote "ring" of our conscious concerns. It remains to be seen whether the U.S. bishops will take up the Pope's challenge and bring his message to the pulpits. It would be an extraordinary act of courage, given the American Church's financial dependence on groups that likely agree with Vance's nationalism—but it's precisely the courage the American Church needs to show.

So, the answer is simply to preach the Gospel, in season and out. But we "preach" the Gospel only by living it, by forming communities within our parishes to do the work the Gospel requires of us. That may be the work of finding fellowship over a beer with our friends at the Knights of Columbus Hall, or joining our local St. Vincent de Paul Society to care for the poor. It means participating in the Mass and the sacraments, and joining our neighbors on civic projects. Either they will know we are Christians by our love, or they won't know it at all. And then, we must find a way to express this love in our politics, our businesses, and our civic lives.

Is there hope for Catholics in American political life? I confess I am not sanguine on this point. The collapse of capitalism, and with it the current world order, does not bode well. But worse — much worse — is the loss of social capital. Indeed, our anger is encouraged and commodified by the oddly named "social" media, a form of communication that is anything but social. And social capital is the foundation of all other types of capital; when it goes, it is difficult to get it back, and difficult for anything to work.

I doubt there is enough time — or interest — in forming small communities (the so-called Benedict Option) to save the situation. And calls for "regime change" seem only to benefit the already powerful. So long as the discussion is confined to small-circulation books or journals, I don't see much hope for our children and grandchildren, except to teach them to be self-reliant. But I could be wrong on this point; it could be that these discussions can become a mustard seed.

Time will tell.

∞ ∞ ∞

JOHN C. MÉDAILLE *teaches theology at the University of Dallas. He is the author of* The Vocation of Business, Toward a Truly Free Market, *and (with Thomas Storck),* Theology: Mythos or Logos?

What We Are Doing vs.
What We Should Be Doing

AL KRESTA

ON THE LAST YEAR, IT HAS FINALLY rushed in on me that the years are ticking past faster than I can remember. Next year, I will have been an active mission-minded Christian for fifty years, and I am grateful for God's guidance and the opportunities that opened up for me. Next year, Sally and I will have been married forty-seven years, with five kids and twenty-one grandkids. Our family culture has been fun, loving, and full of music and laughter, even amid the usual disappointments.

I wish I could say the same for our national political culture. I returned to the Catholic Church in 1992, when John Paul II was pope, and Mother Teresa the most loved woman in the world. When the Jubilee of 2000 arrived, I was overflowing with confidence about the future of the Church in America. The future looked fruitful. I was young then and had focused on the Church's accomplishments. I hadn't read deeply into the darker moments, such as the papacy in the Renaissance. My ignorance had permitted me to be more optimistic than the virtue of hope should have allowed. And then, a short two years later, 9/11 shook up America, and the sex-abuse crisis shook up the Church.

A lot of my optimism was based on the writings of Fr. Richard John Neuhaus, His 1984 book *The Naked Public Square: Religion and Democracy in America*, which I read while I was beginning my pastorate and going to seminary, was life changing. It gave me hope for America and showed me how the Christian faith could make this nation all she was created to be. Christians, I thought, should fight to get a seat at the table whenever activists and politicians gather together. A few years later, Neuhaus's book *The Catholic Moment: The Paradox of the Church in the Postmodern World* continued this positive theme. He believed that the Catholic Church was the only Christian communion with the moral theology, spiritual vocabulary, and social insight to help America flourish.

But, twenty years later, he wrote a much darker book, *American Babylon: Notes From an Exile.* Gradually, I too began to realize that I wasn't living in nineteenth-century pre-Civil War America, where Christian pastors and missionaries worked with Christian entrepreneurs and leaders of academic institutions and pivotal political figures to end slavery or alcohol abuse or promote the distribution of the Scriptures. Back then, we didn't just have a seat at the table; we bought the table and decided who sat there.

Today, however, all the language of getting a seat at the table sounds patronizing and demeaning. Jesus didn't suggest to Matthew or John to get the Apostles a seat at the table with Pilate of Caiaphas. Nor did he tell Jude Thaddeus to beef up his résumé and prepare for tough questions like "You've been studying with this itinerant preacher for the last three years. For what?" To bear witness to a coming kingdom? Sure, okay. Not a great résumé!

All this scrambling to get noticed reminds me of a story told by the late Catholic priest and author Henri Nouwen. Fr. Nouwen was a chaplain on a Holland America cruise liner. One day, while he was on the bridge of the ship, a dangerously thick fog settled in. The steersman could not see the bow, and the captain was pacing nervously while listening to a radar-station operator describe his position between other ships. Fr. Nouwen paced nervously, too, and as he paced, he collided with the captain. The captain cursed the chaplain and told him to stay out of the way.

Fr. Nouwen started to walk away, "filled with feelings of incompetence and guilt," he later wrote in his journal. "But the worst wasn't over. The captain came back and gruffly said: 'Padre, why don't you just stay around. This might be the only time I really need you.'" This priest, this Christian minister, was good for nothing except — maybe — to console the dying after a shipwreck. Christian priests and ministers are helpful only when needed to calm the masses with prayers and other hocus-pocus. But, for crying out loud, keep them off the bridge, out of the map room, and away from the wheel. And keep them out of the corporate boardroom and the congressional chamber, too. As far as the world is concerned, faith is okay; it's kind of like spit. It's good to have a little of it, but keep it to yourself, keep it private. Christianity might be personally meaningful, but it's publicly irrelevant.

Once we start longing for a seat at the table, we forget who we are. Who are we? We are exiles. This world is not our home. We are aliens. Our citizenship is in Heaven. We take our marching orders from a different King. The first papal encyclical begins with these words: "Peter, an apostle of Jesus Christ, to those who are elect exiles of the Dispersion . . . according to the foreknowledge of God the Father, in the sanctification of the Spirit, for obedience to Jesus Christ and for sprinkling with his blood: May grace and peace be multiplied to you."[1] We fool ourselves if we think exiles can set the terms of the cultural debate. I don't think the culture wars have been good for us. Nobody owes us a seat at the table. We should be focused on bearing witness to the age to come.

Robert Louis Wilken, the great American historian of Christianity, now a Catholic, wrote, "In my lifetime we have witnessed the collapse of Christian civilization. At first the process of disintegration was slow, a gradual and persistent attrition, but today it has moved into overdrive, and what is more troubling, it has become deliberate and intentional, not only promoted by the cultured despisers

---

[1] 1 Peter 1:1–2.

of Christianity but often aided and abetted by Christians themselves."[2]

Aided and abetted by Christians themselves. How? Let me give a couple examples.

At eleven o'clock on Sunday morning at The Home Depot, the lines of folks with cans of paint, two-by-fours, and joint cement stretch almost as far as they do on a Saturday morning. The only lingering difference between Sunday and other days of the week is that the malls open later and close earlier. Had Christians united and decided not to shop or work on Sunday except for hardship, what do you think would have happened? Many businesses would have remained closed.

Is this such a big deal? Yes, John Paul II wrote an entire apostolic letter on the proper keeping of the Lord's Day.[3] Unfortunately, most Catholics prefer to act like American consumers than disciples of Jesus. Sunday observance was instituted by God to remind us of His grace and His desire to free us from servile labor so we could care for the sick and the infirm, and so we would be free to cultivate our inner life and strengthen family ties.

Another example. Churchgoing Christians redefined marriage over a few generations. Protestant churches began liberalizing their views on contraception, divorce, and remarriage. Then, as Hollywood began to spin its web of dreams, marriage came to be seen as an institution for adults to find romantic, emotional fulfillment. Gone was the primacy of marriage as an institution that guaranteed the safety, protection, and nurturing of children. Since it was now about the emotional fulfillment of the adult couple, vows started to change from "till death do us part" to "till we decide to part," from "as long as we both shall live" to "as long as we both shall love." Homosexual men and women realized soon that if marriage is principally

---

[2] Robert Louis Wilken, "The Church as Culture," *First Things* (April 2004).

[3] Pope John Paul II, *Dies Domini* (May 31, 1998).

about the romantic feelings of the couple, and children optional or ornamental, they should not be deprived of public recognition of their feelings.

There are but a couple examples of Christians' aping the world and failing to obey St. Paul's clear mandate: "Do not be conformed to this world, but be transformed by the renewal of your mind" (Rom. 12:2).

So, if there is no seat at the table for us Christians, if there is no expectation of "setting the world on fire," then what is our task? Christ has placed us in the middle of the hustle and bustle of daily life to remind men that we live in the light of eternity, that our daily choices render us fit for glory or for damnation. We are here to help people who live in this world of desecration — where human beings are routinely trashed through abortion, war, human trafficking, terrorism, and industrial carelessness — that next to the Eucharist there is nothing more sacred in this world than a human being. We are called to help restore a sense of the sacred to everyday life.

∞ ∞ ∞

AL KRESTA, *formerly CEO of Ave Maria Radio, was best known as the host of the popular radio program* Kresta in the Afternoon. *He succumbed to liver cancer on June 15, 2024. The foregoing is based on a talk he gave, in the last months of his life, at the benefit dinner for a pro-life organization in Ann Arbor, Michigan.*

AFTERWORD
THOMAS STORCK

THE PRESENT BOOK IS A SNAPSHOT of attitudes of American Catholics and some others, including Protestants and non-Christians. Most would identify as *conservative* Christians, though a significant minority would vigorously deny that identification and even dispute the relevance or logical coherence of the term. But it is a snapshot, nonetheless, of attitudes toward the American polity, whatever may be its current trajectory, whether it is on the verge of some sort of greatness or headed into unknown territory or rushing quickly toward ruin. But the writers here are dealing with something deeper than mere political changes, even those that are profound or unexpected. What is happening now, according to one reading of the signs of the times, is that the raw edges of American life are being exposed, and things that have always been present, but have been mostly hidden, are now out in the open; that what has always been implicit in America has become explicit; and that the unraveling of numerous American attitudes and practices—many involving, directly or indirectly, sexual morality, which has been the occasion, if not the cause, of a debate that has deeply divided American society—is simply the unfolding of a trajectory inherent in American life from its beginnings.

But the symposium that was the proximate occasion for this book asks a more direct question: What do Catholics have to do with this polity and the experiment that it is widely held to represent? What attitude ought we to have? And, as readers may see, the answers given here divide themselves broadly into two categories. There are those who are satisfied, even pleased, with the premises upon which this polity and this experiment were founded, either insisting that it is simply the latest iteration of the Church's involvement with the political and social order — an extension even of Christendom — or that the classical liberalism that is part of the air Americans breathe is, or should be, healthy and congenial to Catholics. Then there are those who, basing themselves on papal pronouncements, including the extensive and detailed analyses in Leo XIII's encyclicals of the Church's involvement with the state and the nature of the state itself, take issue with this. Their claim is that, however much the United States has been a haven for persecuted Catholics over time, we can never approve of the fundamental philosophic principles upon which this regime rests, and that in order to achieve public success here, Catholics have always been forced and, absent a massive conversion of both individuals and the culture, always will be forced to exist within a worldview not of our own making.

Such a divergence of attitudes among Catholics is not something new. It was foreshadowed in the early nineteenth century by debates over the relationship of Catholics to the public schools, crystalized in the growing intellectual rift between Fr. Isaac Hecker and Orestes Brownson, and finally became a subject of notable public contention during the Americanist crisis of the 1890s, when prelates such as Archbishop John Ireland of St. Paul, Minnesota, championed an enthusiastic acceptance not only of the American governmental structure but of the cultural climate endemic to this country. The United States, so it was asserted, was especially fertile soil on which the Church might flourish, and it was therefore necessary that Catholic immigrant groups quickly give up their old-world customs and ideas so that they might better adapt themselves to their new home in Protestant America. Only thus could the Church's mission flourish here. This point of view was actively opposed by other prelates, and especially by German-American Catholics, both clergy and some lay journalists. The 1899 letter of Pope Leo to James Cardinal Gibbons, *Testem benevolentiae nostrae*, generally put an end to public debate on the matter, but in practice the Americanist position (as it was termed) more and more became the de facto stance of Catholics in the United States.

With the almost complete breakdown of Catholic discipline following the Second Vatican Council, Catholics have tended to identify simply with one or another of the cultural-political blocs, liberal or conservative as they are called, that dominate American public discourse. Accordingly, probably the majority of politically active Catholics feel more kinship with those non-Catholics who share their commitment to one or the other of these opinion blocs than to Catholics who identify with the opposing bloc. But, in fact, both of these blocs share a basic adherence to American principles and differ only as to what they consider those principles to be. Those who exhibit any reservations about our founding principles, however understood, or about the Church's relationship to them, tend to be politically homeless or to support a minor political movement such as the American Solidarity Party.

The chief importance and value of this volume lies in its making explicit these conflicting viewpoints, in the hope that Catholics here and elsewhere may approach not merely our current political controversies but the fundamental civilizational trends we too often take for granted with greater awareness and insight into what is actually at stake and the implications of the alternate paths that are open to us.